Writing the Western Landscape

Other volumes in The Concord Library
Series Editor: John Elder

Eighty Acres: Elegy for a Family Farm
Ronald Jager

Tarka the Otter
Henry Williamson

The Insect World of J. Henri Fabre
Edwin Way Teale, editor

A Land
Jacquetta Hawkes

In Limestone Country
Scott Russell Sanders

Nature and *Walking*
Ralph Waldo Emerson and Henry David Thoreau

Following the Bloom
Douglas Whynott

Finding Home: Writing on Nature and Culture from Orion *Magazine*
Peter Sauer, editor

The Very Rich Hours: Travels in Orkney, Belize, the Everglades, and Greece
Emily Hiestand

Thoreau on Birds
Francis H. Allen, editor

Staying Put: Making a Home in a Restless World
Scott Russell Sanders

The Geography of Childhood: Why Children Need Wild Places
Gary Paul Nabhan and Stephen Trimble

Family of Earth and Sky: Indigenous Tales of Nature from around the World
John Elder and Hertha Wong, editors

MARY AUSTIN *and* JOHN MUIR

Writing the

Western

Landscape

Edited, introduced, and illustrated by Ann H. Zwinger

BEACON PRESS • BOSTON

Beacon Press
25 Beacon Street
Boston, Massachusetts 02108-2892

Beacon Press books are published under the auspices
of the Unitarian Universalist Association of Congregations.

99 98 97 96 95 94   8 7 6 5 4 3 2 1

Text design by David Bullen
Composition by Wilsted & Taylor
Library of Congress Cataloging-in-Publication Data
Austin, Mary Hunter, 1868–1934.
Writing the Western landscape / Mary Austin and John Muir;
edited, introduced, and illustrated by Ann H. Zwinger.
p.   cm. — (Concord library)
Includes bibliographical references (p.   ).
ISBN 0-8070-8526-X
1. Natural history—West (U.S.)—Literary collections.
2. Landscape—West (U.S.)—Literary collections.
3. Nature—Literary collections.   I. Muir, John, 1838–1914.
II. Zwinger, Ann.   III. Title.   IV. Series.
PS3501.U8A6   1994
508.78—dc20   94-9139

Contents

Introduction by Ann H. Zwinger

vii

PART I: MARY AUSTIN

Earth Horizon: Autobiography, selections

3

The Land of Journeys' Ending, selections

45

PART II: JOHN MUIR

The Grand Cañon of the Colorado

89

Travels in Alaska, selections

119

Introduction

In 1904 Mary Austin described her only meeting with John Muir:

There was no town at Carmel then; nothing but a farm or two, one or two graceless buildings, and the wild beach and the sunny dunes. In the meantime, "The Land of Little Rain" was published and had a great success. Mary was at the Hittells' for that and got to know the elect: Miss [Ina] Coolbrith, Charles Warren Stoddard, who was living then at Monterey, John Muir, William Keith, and [Edwin] Markham. Of all these I recall John Muir the most distinctly, a tall lean man with the habit of talking much, the habit of soliloquizing. He told stories of his life in the world, and of angels; angels that saved him; that lifted and carried him; that showed him where to put his feet; he believed them. I told him one of mine: except that I didn't see mine. I had been lifted and carried; I had been carried out of the way of danger; and he believed me. I remember them still.

The paragraph from *Earth Horizon*, Austin's autobiography, with its peculiar mixture of first and third person, tells much about both of them. In 1904 Muir was sixty-six, already a legend, the model for the hero of a current popular novel, known for conservation work that included founding the Sierra Club and cham-

Introduction

pioning national park status for Yosemite, and had more writing and speaking projects than an ordinary person could handle. He had only another decade to live. Muir had essentially proved what he was going to prove while Austin at thirty-six had a whole lifetime of work ahead. Austin was a newcomer, savoring the good reviews of her first book, *The Land of Little Rain*, and in the process of freeing herself from an incompatible marriage and pursuing the writer's life in the heady atmosphere of Carmel and San Francisco.

Austin's voice is that of a woman making her way in a world generally unsupportive of single women; it was too early in her career to know how writing would round and fill her life. As a woman who preferred being the center of attention, she is upstaged by Muir's exuberance and makes a point of being unimpressed by the darling of California writers and conservationists: if Muir could have angels, so could she.

Muir came to his guardian angels through a stern biblical upbringing which he happily and pragmatically managed to reconcile with the evolutionary theories of Darwin and the commands of natural science. Crossing a glacier,

I was suddenly brought to a dead stop, with arms outspread, clinging close to the face of the rock, unable to move hand or foot either up or down. My doom appeared fixed. I *must* fall. . . . I became nerve-shaken for the first time since setting foot on the mountains, and my mind seemed to fill with a stifling smoke. But this terrible eclipse lasted only a moment, when life blazed forth again with preternatural clearness. I seemed suddenly to become possessed of a new sense. The other self, bygone experiences, Instinct, or Guardian Angel — call it what you

Introduction

will — came forward and assumed control . . . and my limbs moved with
a positiveness and precision with which I seemed to have nothing at all
to do. Had I been borne aloft upon wings, my deliverance could not
have been more complete.

Austin's sense of clairvoyance had its source in equally dramatic
circumstances: although miles away, she received a vision of her
mother at the moment of her death. In San Francisco she was
"oppressed with an impending sense of disaster" the day before
the 1906 earthquake hit.

Both acknowledged and trusted that "other self." Their mys-
tical communication with the natural world places both writers
in the Transcendentalist tradition of the East Coast writers
whom they most revered, Ralph Waldo Emerson and Henry David Thoreau.

When Emerson visited Yosemite in 1871, Muir was in his
early thirties, so shy he scarcely had the courage to speak to
someone he esteemed so greatly. After talking with Muir, Emerson returned the regard and placed Muir's name on a limited list
of those he most admired. Although Austin never met Emerson,
she paid homage to him in her autobiography: "Oddly, the only
writer out of those days who affected her style was Emerson. I
don't know why. The predilection showed itself early in her college life. Possibly his death in '82 had revived public attention in
his work, and that in turn had recalled associations with her father, among whose books she had found an early edition of the
'Poems,' and 'Representative Men.'"

Austin may have been indebted to Emerson's words, and Muir

Introduction

venerated Emerson and regarded Thoreau as the wisest of them all, yet Austin and Muir departed sharply from the way in which the East Coast writers viewed and wrote about the world around them. The two johnny-come-lately westerners took the conventions of eastern natural history writing literally and figuratively into new territory and in so doing made a statement that was particularly and emphatically western.

Both Muir and Austin are the first truly *western* nature writers. They delineate the personality of pine and spruce, describe the delicious sibilance of sand, portray the palatial grandeur of glaciers, divine the cut of the wind and the shocking immensity of sky that it swirls out of. They celebrate landscape as animate, existing on its own, requiring no explanation, no intellectualization, only devotion, insight, and understanding. Their writing, their point of view, their dedication to the mountains and deserts of the West, has sustained western nature writers from their day forward.

Since landscape and the natural world form their subject, the genesis of their dramatic confrontation and identification with the land bears directly on what and how they wrote. The distinctive attitude that Austin and Muir brought to the western landscape came about through a felicitous combination of circumstances, most notably the accident of their discovery, in their young adulthood, of a landscape that was completely different from the ones in which they had grown up, and that they embraced and adopted with the intensity of lost children finding home. Austin's unfolding knowledge of the desert, and Muir's of

Introduction

the mountains, focused, enriched, absorbed, and challenged them both.

Austin grew up in the flat farmlands of Illinois. She followed her older brother to Blackburn College where she pursued a study program in science even though she knew she would be a writer: "English I can study by myself; for science I have to have laboratories and a teacher." Out of her work in science came her "consuming interest" in botany. In 1888 her brother decided to homestead in California, and as soon as Austin graduated the family moved to Tejon Valley. The family camped on the way west and continued to do so while waiting for permanent quarters. By good chance they found a place near the huge El Tejon Ranch south of Bakersfield owned by General Edward Fitzgerald Beale, who had made the first (and last) transit of the United States with camels. Beale, then in his sixties and somewhat of a local celebrity, was enchanted by Austin's interest in the environs and its history, and she, at twenty, was enthralled by his store of knowledge, his generosity, and his respect for her intellect she felt emphatically missing from her family (according to Austin, her mother never evinced "the smallest interest" in Austin's writing). It was the beginning of her devotion to western vistas: "None other than this long brown land lays such a hold on the affections. The rainbow hills, the tender bluish mists, the luminous radiance of the spring, have the lotus charm. They trick the sense of time, so that once inhabiting there you always mean to go away without quite realizing that you have not done it." Three years later she married Wallace Austin and moved to the Owens Valley which she would celebrate in *The Land of Little Rain*.

Introduction

As a child Muir migrated with his family from a hard life in Scotland to a hard life in Wisconsin. He labored on the family farm far beyond the limits of normal endurance, underwent almost daily beatings for work not accomplished or biblical passages not committed to memory: "If we failed in any part, however slight, we were whipped; for the grand, simple, all-sufficing Scotch discovery had been made that there was a close connection between the skin and the memory, and that irritating the skin excited the memory to any required degree." Despite having no formal education between the time he came to Wisconsin at eleven until he went to college at twenty-two, Muir shone as a student at the newly established University of Wisconsin. He supported himself by his ingenious inventions (among his designs, an alarm clock that would tilt the bed upright and jar him awake in the black of night). He discovered botany and became obsessed with plant collecting "in wild enthusiasm . . . [and] my eyes never closed on the plant glory I had seen."

He left the University of Wisconsin for his own "University of the Wilderness" where, like Bernard of Clairvaux seven centuries before him, he would learn more from trees and stones than he would from books and teachers. He first went to Canada where he collected voraciously and continued to earn his living through his inventions and hard work. In 1867, when the mill in which he worked burned, he returned to the United States. An accident on the job in Indianapolis convinced Muir of his life's work. A piece of wood flew in his right eye and for days he feared he would be blind. While recovering he resolved to devote the rest of his life to studying nature. As soon as his eye healed, he be-

Introduction

gan a southeastward walk, through lands recently ravaged by the Civil War, protected only by his intelligence and charm. He undertook his "thousand-mile walk" to Florida, contracted malaria there, decided his plans to continue to South America were too extravagant both for his pocketbook and his health, and shipped to Cuba instead. His enchantment with this foreign country sparked a life-long wanderlust, a condition he characterized as being "doomed to be 'carried of the spirit of the wilderness.'" The next year he booked passage to California, arriving in April 1868. He found the Oakland Hills bedizened with flowers and the air "quivering with sunshine and lark song." Within a fortnight he strode into the Sierra Nevada where the notched and ragged mountain horizons captivated his mind and heart, and where he would spend the next six years. He was twenty-nine.

It is perhaps idle to speculate whether either Muir or Austin could have written with such immediacy and intensity about the shuttered forests and quiet ponds and cultivated terrains of their childhoods. But it is not idle to mark that the vistas to which they came by simple chance in their young adulthood were dramatically different, majestic and commanding landscapes unlike anything either of them grew up with in Wisconsin or Illinois. The desert and mountains were harsh environments that left their mark on the biota as well as the psyche, lands that sheltered plants and animals stringently adapted to a severe world, living on the edge of survival. The harshness of the habitats they wrote about repelled many, especially in a turn-of-the-century culture intent upon taming them, but this antinature attitude goaded

Introduction

Austin and Muir to pioneer their distinctive way of seeing the world on their own terms.

For western natural history writers today, as well as for Muir and Austin, the catalyst was the grandeur of the landscape itself, operatic, commanding and demanding, rugged and raw and glorious. Western desert and mountain panoramas are sweeping, awesome in scale. They are brilliantly lit, crisply defined. The evidence of disaster and cataclysm lurk everywhere: volcanism, wild fires, catastrophic storms, treacherous aridity—people in the West live next door to or on top of geologic and natural mayhem.

The fragile alpine forget-me-not blooms beneath a brilliant blue and all-encompassing sky and endures a desperate climate. The delicate evening-primrose withstands the sand-dune dryness and flourishes. Apple green map lichen, creating a territory measured in centimeters, stakes out its geography on a wall a thousand feet high. Minute dark green mosses thrive in the tiny cracks of granite slabs as big as train stations. It is a confusing landscape, for wherever there is delicate detail, there is also monumentality of scale without the middle ground one needs for human measurement. In the dry, clear air, faraway objects seem comfortably close and turn out to be amazingly distant. Compare Mt. Katahdin with Mt. Whitney, Walden Pond with the Great Salt Lake, and the immensity of the contrast in scale is inescapable.

Muir and Austin responded to these powerful landscapes, and their elegant descriptions present a priceless baseline of what the natural world of California was and underline the necessity for maintaining the health of these places. As nature writers in the West, they established the veracity of an immediate relationship to the landscape and made it obvious at the outset that the landscape and learning about it is subject enough.

One of the ways in which Muir and Austin came to grips with a new and overwhelming landscape was to remain out *in* it for extended periods of time. Heretofore people who spent time away from civilization generally did so by the necessity of their trade: hunters and trappers, traders, miners, guides, all those who had to travel long distances that precluded returning to the comfort of a home in town at night. To "camp out," to deliberately seek the isolation of nights away from civilization, was just beginning to be a conceptual possibility.

Both Emerson and Thoreau walked a ruderal landscape. They surveyed stone walls and trimmed garden paths rather than climbing granite walls or hiking a waterless desert. They gazed on vistas framed with trees whose curtains of leaves screened grazed pastures and mowed sedge meadows only rods away, under a sky softened by Atlantic Coast humidity, as if a scrim intervened between the observer and the keen clarity of the landscape. In the philosopher's solutions and solitudes, abstracting landscape into another level of understanding, Emerson seems almost to separate himself from the landscape he loved. Thoreau, younger, more outdoors-oriented, did hike miles of mountains and trails, but mostly he sauntered through settled countryside.

Easterners often could not relate to the immensity of landscape in the West. On his visit to California, instead of exploring

Introduction

the magnificent scenery of Yosemite, Emerson and his companions spent lunchtime reciting Sir Walter Scott and discussing Boccaccio. The ever-enthusiastic Muir, eager to share his world, proposed an overnight in the mountains. When Emerson's companions overruled it, Muir judged that they were too "full of indoor philosophy" and berated their "dread of pure night air, though it is only cooled day air with a little dew in it. So the carpet dust and unknowable reeks were preferred. And to think of this being a Boston choice. Sad commentary on culture and the glorious transcendentalism." Reacting as people still do today when overwhelmed and disoriented by scale, Emerson's companions simply took refuge in the known and familiar, and eschewed the new and unfamiliar.

Although Thoreau did camp out, it was nearly always within earshot of civilization, and he did not court the twenty-four-hour outdoor experience throughout his life as Muir did. The cabin at Walden Pond was simple living, yes, but it had a sturdy roof and was close enough to go home to mother's for dinner.

Staying out under the stars has many advantages. Only then can there be the pleasure of sunrise when the sky brightens and day begins to breathe, as well as the comfort of sunset and shadows sweeping across a terrain slowly being absorbed by darkness. The wanderer becomes attuned to night sounds and to day aromas that are masked in town. Nobody likes to be caught cold, wet, tired, and hungry, yet the irony is that being so brings out qualities of endurance, fosters concentrated observation, deepens one's experience, and rearranges one's relationship to the

Introduction

natural world — and all this generates a different approach to writing. Survival puts a different edge on things.

In Muir's and Austin's days there were no down sleeping bags, no lightweight rip-stop nylon tents, no dried food to lighten a pack, and most people were still too close to the dark and threatening forests and to the fears of crossing the desert or the mountains to think that bivouacking had any virtue; indeed, it was more likely to be avoided like the plague. Sleeping out-of-doors the way Muir did — "I am often out alone for weeks where you couldn't find me" — with only a marginal food supply allowed him to journey far afield, to stay and to study, with only the most tenuous tether to civilization. Muir's youthful habits of eating little and completing long hours of farm labor preconditioned him to long strenuous walks on nothing more than a cup of tea and a thick slab of bread, stamina that wore out many less hardy companions. For Muir, "going out, I found, was really going in."

Camping was one of only two pastimes (the other was amateur theatricals) that Austin enjoyed with her husband, Wallace, and when she could not be out overnight she was out every minute of daylight she could manage. Although mountains were close by — and there are descriptions of alpine habitats in *The Land of Little Rain* — because of family responsibilities Austin could seldom go far from home, but could wander the desert daily. And she knew the desert at night: "It is hard to escape the sense of mastery as the stars move in the wide clear heavens to risings and settings unobscured. They look large and near and palpitant; as if they moved on some stately service not needful to declare. Wheeling

Introduction

to their stations in the sky, they make the poor world-fret of no account. Of no account you who lie out there watching, nor the lean
coyote that stands off in the scrub from you and howls and
howls."

So many parallels exist in the lives of Austin and Muir that it is
tempting to write about them in parallel: childhoods difficult to
outright abusive, coming to and embracing a new landscape in
their adulthood, the poignant loss of places they held dear to
water development interests — Muir seeing his beloved Hetch
Hetchy dammed to provide water for San Francisco development, Austin watching the verdant Owens Valley turned to alkali
desert by the rapacious Los Angeles Water Board. In Austin's
case, being a woman in the late nineteenth and early twentieth
centuries carried with it all the Victorian baggage of "nice girls
don't," and one of the things nice girls didn't was camp out alone
or be too intelligent, a state of affairs Austin describes poignantly
in her autobiography:

Moreover, Susie [Austin's mother] had taken pains to impress upon her
the childish character of her interest in nature and the inexpedience of
talking about it. . . . You must not quote; especially poetry and Thoreau. An occasional light reference to Burroughs was permissible, but
not Thoreau. A very little experience demonstrated that Susie was
right. You gathered that outdoors as a subject of conversation was boring to most people.

Nor did Austin have the freedom to travel far afield that Muir, not
subject to the same societal strictures, and released for months at

Introduction

a time from family responsibilities by a preternaturally accommodating wife, enjoyed.

She was further trammeled by needing to support her family, for Wallace Austin's schemes continually failed and he often refused to work if the job didn't suit him. Austin's only child, Ruth, developed severe behavioral problems. Mary Austin, with no caring support in an impossible situation, lacking the skills and techniques to care for an often-violent child, was nevertheless condemned by her peers when she placed Ruth in a mental hospital in 1905 (Ruth died there at the age of twenty-eight in the flu epidemic of 1918).

Within her limitations, when endowed with the respectability her status as a young married woman gave her, Mary Austin roamed the environs of Lone Pine, the small town in California at the northern end of the Owens Valley where her husband had a teaching position. At the foot of Mt. Whitney, due west of Death Valley and separated from it by the Inyo Mountains, she came to know the people of both the deserts and the arid foothills, the Basque sheepherders like those she had known near El Tejon, and the Indians who accepted her and taught her their knowledge of healing herbs and, when Austin was ill, helped care for her and her child. In later life, Austin championed the cultures of the indigenous people who lived in the desert, praised their baskets and pottery and culture.

Those blocks of time in the open air stamped Austin's thinking and writing. Austin knew "that all she needed was to be alone with [nature] for uninterrupted occasions, in which they might come to terms." In taking every advantage of what she *could* do,

Introduction

she learned and penned a portrait of environments and people alien to most, and uncovered a signal beauty in a landscape disdained by many. In the desert Austin found respite from and reflection of the bleakness of her marriage. She imbued an arid environment most people judged desolate with the beauty she found there. She countered the desolation she felt in her own life both with the harmonious ways of people who had lived there for centuries and with knowledge of a flora and fauna exquisitely adapted to place. When the Los Angeles Water Board usurped the water in the Owens Valley and piped it to a greedy city, the valley's subsequent desiccation left Austin feeling that "there was nothing more for her in Southern California," and she left.

Mary Austin was a writer first and a naturalist second, which is not to say that she was not remarkably well qualified as a naturalist. She was an alert and perceptive observer, a knowledgeable listener to the desert, and a keen taster of the wind. Well educated for her time, full of insatiable curiosity, from childhood on she always knew that writing came first. She trafficked with the literary and artistic lights of the day like Jack London and Ansel Adams, traveled several times to Europe, lived in and complained about New York for many years but did not leave until she received the recognition she felt her due.

Austin had no agent so was forced to promote herself, difficult for any artist to do, and was eternally concerned about money. Supporting herself meant keeping up a killing lecture schedule that cut into her writing time. Despite this, she was a prolific writer, publishing around two hundred pieces in more than sixty-five periodicals, more than thirty books (of which a dozen

Introduction

were nonfiction), novels, short stories and poems, children's books, and three plays. The incessant writing projects necessary to keep her afloat financially meant that much of the work not founded in the natural world sometimes falters, seems forced and convoluted. Resentments frequently crowd her work. Austin felt, justly or unjustly, that her mother was neglectful and indifferent to the point of mistreatment (one cannot help but compare Austin's smoldering bitterness toward her mother with that of Muir toward his father, a physically abusive and psychologically destructive man: Muir survived and went beyond and never gave way to rancor while Austin's disaffections snake through her work).

Eventually Austin settled in Santa Fe, New Mexico, where she was back again beside the desert. Here Austin knew a company of like women, strong, often difficult, certainly talented, who chose to live and/or work in the Southwest, women like Georgia O'Keeffe, Laura Gilpin, Willa Cather, Mabel Dodge Luhan. Here she found support for her feminist views in the invigorating presence of these women artists and writers and in an ambiance that was beginning to acknowledge the abilities and power of the female mind. Austin died in Santa Fe in 1934.

Muir was a naturalist first, a writer second. By impeccable, painstaking research, he found irrefutable evidence of glaciation in the Yosemite Valley and challenged the leading geological minds of the day who clung to their erroneous notion that Sierra Nevada's valleys had been formed by subsidence. Through those long hours of observation, Muir came to an understanding of the

Introduction

unique fragility of the West and developed a philosophy of conservation.

Muir, who never planned to be a writer, turned out to be an uncommonly fine one, with a clarity of observation and an enthusiasm of expression. He combined a charming persona and outdoor knowledge with a delightful, lilting style. He became, more by accident than intent, a nature writer's nature writer. Mary Austin's brief description of Muir catches the outstanding qualities of his personality, his deep religious beliefs, and his prolixity. That Muir's exuberance occasionally gets out of hand is due both to a more florid mode of expression popular in Muir's day and to an overabundance of ardor that was part and parcel of an energetic personality. At its worst his writing is verbose; at its best it retains an artlessness and directness, the nature writer's childlike openness and enthusiasm. Muir becomes the gentle guide one wants to follow (by comparison, Austin often seems to lecture).

Muir's writing reflects years of letter writing in which he honed his skills of narration and clear, concise expression. He was an indefatigable and vivid correspondent, keeping in close touch with friends and a beloved family, narrating his journeys and his studies:

Here is a clean white-skinned glacier from the back of McClure with glassy emerald flesh and singing crystal blood, all bright and pure as a sky, yet handling mud and stone like a navvy, building moraines like a plodding Irishman. Here is a cascade two hundred feet wide, half a mile long, glancing this way and that, filled with bounce and dance and joyous hurrah, yet earnest as a tempest, and singing like angels loose on a frolic from heaven.

If Austin's mother found her daughter's work "beyond" her, Muir's fundamentalist father denied his son's work because it was "not doing God's work," and "the best and soonest way of getting quit of the writing and publishing your book is to burn it, and then it will do no more harm either to you or to others." Happily, later in life Muir's father had a conversion and became the most loving of fathers.

Where Austin consorted with other writers, Muir consorted with scientists. His work on glaciers brought him the enjoyable company of John Tyndall, an eminent English authority on glaciers, and of botanists Asa Gray and John Torrey. In 1903 he guided Theodore Roosevelt into the mountains, a trip that would culminate in Congress's receding Yosemite to become a national park.

After six years in Yosemite, Muir left, having lost the battle for Hetch Hetchy, "satisfied to leave all and labor in other fields," and began his roamings over the earth. He toured Egypt, Siberia, the Philippines, China, and almost everywhere in between, including several trips to Alaska to study the glaciers there.

In a life busy managing the family orchards, lecturing, writing, traveling, Muir never got around to writing his planned autobiography, which says something about his outer focus. When he speaks of himself it is usually with self-effacing and charming

Introduction

humor. He had no regrets and resentments to exorcise, having long since forgiven his father with a generosity that is almost beyond understanding. *The Story of My Boyhood and Youth* ends when he went to the University of Wisconsin, and never continues, although he lived a long life, dying in 1914. He found it always more interesting to write about the natural world than about himself.

Both Muir and Austin achieved instant recognition with their first writings, Austin with *The Land of Little Rain* published in 1903 and Muir with *The Mountains of California*, a compilation of essays written over sixteen years that did not appear until 1894 when Muir was in his forties. That they continued to write their pleasure in and obligation to the natural world marks them as focused natural history writers, devoted to the discipline.

Through their work they awaken the reader to the joys of discovering the landscape, to the bombardier beetle that stalks the desert and the tiny primroses that grace an alpine fell, to ouzels that prance the waterways, to storms that rise up like avenging angels onto the mountain peaks and cut a new arroyo in the desert. Out of their pages come the roar of winter in the mountains and the blaze of summer in the desert. They made the landscapes about which they wrote so much their own that one cannot walk the Owens Valley or New Mexican desert, or hike the Sierra Nevadas or view an Alaskan glacier, without heeding their awakening to the sumptuousness of the natural world.

Austin personalized the desert as a metaphor for her life, and in being there found the saving health and inspiration she

Introduction

needed. The very qualities of the desert that most people found unacceptable, its aridity and bleakness and its importunate demands, its dangers, made for stunning and arresting beauty, and the desert brought a healing she craved. Muir found God's hand everywhere. He transcended the landscape he loved and passed through to another level, a system of ethics that galvanized people to care for the landscape and colored their reactions to mountainscapes ever after.

In their mature work both returned to the source of their earliest writing and in so doing tapped into the eternal youthfulness and enthusiasm available to those who find their inspiration in the natural world. Their joy and delight lies in the austerity of ice and the translucency of poppy petal, in the exhilarating diversity of the natural world where, as Muir recorded, the pull of place is the most important grace: "Camp out among the grass and gentians of glacier meadows, in craggy garden nooks full of Nature's darlings. Climb the mountains and get their good tidings. Nature's peace will flow into you as sunshine flows into trees. The winds will blow their own freshness into you, and the storms their energy, while cares will drop off like autumn leaves."

Editor's Note In truth, the selections from Muir and Austin chose themselves. As I read through the works of each, certain passages requested marking, and invariably these were the ones I finally chose for this book—writing that to me epitomized the character of these two western writers and selections that were serendipitous comparisons.

I deliberately did not choose selections from the best-known

Introduction

work, from Muir's *Mountains of California* or from Austin's *The Land of Little Rain*, and concentrated on works less often read. Out of this tremendous number of words and innumerable paragraphs, a picture began to emerge of what Wallace Stegner (and many others) have talked about as the western idiom of writing. For me, that was narrowed further to natural history writing, and only in a wide perusal of Muir's and Austin's work did I come to appreciate the tremendous contribution their western point of view made to natural history writing and how these paths diverged not in a woods but in the mountains and the deserts. With the East/West difference in mind, passages continuously emerged that reinforced the thesis of a distinctive western viewpoint fostered by an extraordinary western landscape.

In the reading, I could not help but remark the leaner style of today's nature writing and the glorious amount of scientific research available to today's writers. Often I had the feeling that both Muir and Austin could have used a canny editor doing some gentle, perceptive trimming. But Muir and Austin wrote for a different time with a wider readership, not competing with flashier means of communication, a luxury today's nature writers probably don't have. Today's western nature writers walk the broad path between Muir's story-telling ebullience and occasional lack of substance and Austin's insistence on substance and research that sometimes damped an open radiance of expression. Those of us working today are better writers because Muir and Austin walked the edges.

Mary Austin

Earth Horizon

Autobiography

*P*ublished in 1932, Mary Austin's autobiography, Earth Horizon, *was her next-to-last book. It delineates both her life as a writer and her developing devotion to the natural world which proved her salvation, as both woman and writer. Frequently it is a litany of real and imagined resentments, name-dropping, and is marred with a galloping and imperious self-absorption. Nevertheless, the book is an invaluable window into a writer's personality as well as an encapsulation of the life and times of artistic women of the early twentieth century. It was one of her few commercial successes.*

Austin is open, sometimes confrontationally so, about her life, and her quirks of style are intriguing. The revealed personality—not the persona that she perhaps planned to present but the one that comes through—is strong, focused, often difficult, always centered on self and on writing. Austin loved to hear herself write.

These selections from Earth Horizon *begin with Austin's early awareness of her different-ness and her calling to be a writer, followed by the poignant loss of her father and of her younger sister, Jennie, the only person whom she felt loved her "unselflessly." The family journey west after her graduation brings her into contact with the dazzling western landscape where, despite a disastrous marriage and an unruly child, Austin wrote her first book about the desert and entered into the literary life.*

*O*n this occasion, she remembers perfectly how beautifully Jennie's robe flowed over Father's arm. The day was warm; the hill loomed enormously. Mary wilted down in the middle of the boardwalk. Father made a gesture of passing the baby to Mother, to pick up his older daughter.

"Let her alone," said Mother. "She'll come when she finds she has to." And to Mary, "Look at Jim, he's not complaining," which was too familiar an admonition for Mary to realize that it was also unfair, since Jim was already well on the road to five. Feeling very small and faint, she sat on the hot boardwalk and saw the rest of the family disappear over the top of the hill. Mary never doubted that she was abandoned. She lay under the weight of that certainty without motion or sound, an event not to be coped with. Finally over the hill a figure appeared, it drew near . . . Papa! The recollection snaps off like a broken stick. What I suspect is that the instant relief appeared, Mary laid her head on the boardwalk and went to sleep. I've known her to do things like that.

One other instance has no date, but since it undoubtedly occurred on First South Street, was either in her second spring or late the same autumn. She was out-of-doors, blue and a flicker of color overhead. Jennie was in the cradle—a low hooded cradle with solid rockers easy to move about, as distinguished from the crib-cradle to which you were promoted as soon as you ceased to be *the* baby. Outside, beyond the cradle's rim, pale round flowers in the grass. Bindweed! Mary knew that was what you called it . . . pale films of color fluttering, and a feeling that went with it . . . it was a long time before you got a name for the feeling, but bindweed you never forgot. Only—this was very odd—when the recollection came back to you, there was sometimes a singular confusion, the bindweed was always there, but it was Mary in the cradle, and Jennie did not come into the picture at all. So it is just possible that Mary was less than two years old when it occurred — bindweed has a long season of blooming and proves nothing.

The only thing worth noting in all these is that they occurred out-of-doors. Not, as it was afterward proved, that there weren't other things remembered out of the first two and a half years, but these were the only things that spontaneously recurred to mind.

One incident of the hegira from First South Street, marked for Mary the beginning of a series of occurrences which was to become the source of a good deal of bewilderment and blame from which she was never able to extricate herself. Brother Jim, in virtue of his status of "going-on-six," had been permitted to ride to the new home on the last load of goods, which he fell off of going down Mayo's Hill, and without making any outcry had managed to scramble back on the way up the next; an exploit which lacked something of the fine flavor of success which he imagined for it when Mother discovered how much of the spring mud had scrambled back with him. Nevertheless, it was an exploit which deserved re-telling, but the mistake Mary made was in telling it as something she had seen. Mother set her right. To say that you'd seen things when you hadn't was storying, and storying was wicked. But you did see it; you shut your eyes and there it was as plain as plain, Jim sitting on the mattress on the back of the wagon, down Mayo's Hill between the huge white house on one side and the rail fence with the wild-plum thicket on the other.

"You just imagined it," said Mother.

Mary Austin

"What is 'magine, Mama?"

"Thinking you see things when you don't."

But how could you? And how did you know the difference between seeing and thinking you had seen? It seemed to be always happening; grown-ups thought it funny, but Jim, who was a stern moralist, after the way of brothers where their sisters are concerned, told on you, and Mother said she supposed she'd have to punish you or you would grow up a story-teller. Well, you *did* see them. If you got punished for it, you'd simply have to stand it. . . .

It was in these years before events began to happen one after the other, while Mary was between three and a half and five and a half, that the roots of trouble showed themselves, had to be reckoned with, and to her small capacity overcome. It began as I have described with her not always knowing whether she had seen things, in the sense that other people saw them, or hadn't. It had something to do with the quality of experience. Whether it happened in a picture, in a book, or in a story she was told, either it flashed instantly into a picture, or it didn't. And the picture stayed. According to the degree of her interest in it, it stayed to the minutest detail! — the form and especially the color and feeling that went with it. It was perhaps the intensity of feeling evoked which accounted for the conviction that the event in question took place in her presence — Great-Grandmother Polly being carried off by the Indians, the wolves snuffling under the puncheon floor at the minister's children, the slain on battlefields crawling in heaps — they *happened* to her. After Mary learned how wicked it was, as well as annoying to your parents, to talk about things as though you had been there when you hadn't, she made for herself a criterion of distinction which served in most cases. If you saw things the way other people meant seeing, you saw all around them, matching up with houses, people, earth, and sky, you saw them as *belonging*. But if the picture failed to match, if around the edges of the event you found ragged fringes of grayness, the chances were that you had *imagined* something you had only heard about. In general this worked, but not always. To this day there are a few of these recalled images which she is not sure about.

And then there were dreams. Until you found yourself laughed at, you supposed they really must have happened; and then you discovered that dreams had a way of fading out, murky and yellow at the edges. Still, there were a lot of things — like the Great Snow. When Mary was a child, there were still people in Carlinville who dated things from the Great Snow in '36, when the flakes fell fifteen feet deep on the level, and men driving their hogs to market in Alton had to dump out their wagon-loads of corn and fodder and abandon the hogs to make the best of it; only to find them, after the thaw, piled on one another for warmth, frozen stiff where they stood. Or Annie Pritchard who married and set out barefoot on her wedding journey to Ohio — you looked at old Annie Pritchard and wondered how she could ever have been young enough to have a wedding. By dint of attaching these things to the teller of them, Aunt Sally, or Grandma Berry, you arrived at notions of reality distributed in time.

There was another dreadful difficulty which Mary was always getting into, which she was never able to correct because there was never any way of knowing in advance when it was going to happen. Mary said things; unaccountable, inexcusable things that annoyed visitors. She would be sitting in her little chair, being a good child according to prescription, which determined that good children, when there was company, should be seen and not heard, and suddenly in a lull in the conversation out they would come, the things that simply should not have been said; things about people, the way they felt; the reasons, generally inadmissible, for doing this or that; the things going on in people's minds, of what they carefully weren't talking about. No particular instance occurs; not knowing she was going to say it, Mary didn't always know, until she was confronted with the general consternation, that she *had*. Nor had she any notion why it should prove so annoying. She was scolded about it; she was punished; Mother sometimes shed tears of pure vexation; sometimes she said, "I think the child is possessed." She said people would think she had been gossiping and Mary had repeated what she had heard, though the truth was that nothing was further from Susie's habit of mind than gossip. Not one of her children ever heard her say an unkind or misrepresentative thing about anybody.

Pressed to explain her transgression, Mary said it was like a little bird that hopped out of her mind, onto her tongue, before she could stop it. When she was older she began to realize that it was as if a hidden spring in her mind had been freed by something noted, a look, a tone, something so slight that before it could be named the spring was off, and out had hopped the little bird. Subjected to parental disapprobation, Mary wept, promised not to do it again; and did it. To this day, let her come into a room where there is a situation being saved, a secret antagonism guarded, and unless she is warned by expecting something of the kind, Mary in the first half-minute can quite innocently explode the whole works. Sometimes if she feels, without being able to put her finger on it, guile working underground, she can release the hidden spring herself, and with the flick of the little bird's tail, all the card houses come toppling to the table, for anyone to pick out the winning one as he is able.

How much of this came before, or after the arrival of I-Mary there is no recalling. She came so suddenly and always so inevitably that I doubt if anybody ever knew about her, or could have been made to understand. This would have been a few months after Mary had passed her fourth birthday. Jim had turned six in July and in September was invested with a primer and started to the public school. He started to school with Pa, going to his office in the morning, and home in the late afternoon, but on blustery days such as this, he was kept in the house. Mother was kneading the bread and Jim was studiously reciting his ABC's. At the other corner of the bread board, Mary was busy with a bit of pinched off dough and looking over his shoulder. "A," said Jim, and "O." "O," said Mary, making her mouth the shape of the mark. Presently Jim pointed out "I." "Eye?" said Mary, plumping one floury finger on her own. "No," said Mother, "I, myself, *I* want a drink, I-Mary."

"I-Mary."

Something turned over inside her; the picture happened. There was the familiar room, the flurry of snow outside; Mama kneading bread; Jim with his molasses-colored hair "roached" on top, so that the end of the curl fell over in the middle of his fore-head; Mary in her flannel frock and blue chambray pinafore, on her stool at the corner of the board . . . how small her hand looked beside Mama's . . . the grimy bit of dough rolled out like a worm. . . . And inside her, I-Mary, looking on. I-Mary, I-Mary, *I-Mary!*

Always until she was quite grown up, I-Mary was associated with the pages of books. The mere sight of the printed page would often summon her, and since her coming was comfortably felt — there was a reason for that which comes next — it was sought in the contemplation of print. Mary insisted on being shown every-thing in Jim's primer. Jim liked showing it, even when he had to resort to authority for the exact meaning of what he showed. Thereafter, if Mary found a picture in a book with printing under it, she demanded to be told what it said. When stories were read her, she was never happy until she had got the page in hand and stared hard at it. I-Mary didn't always come out of it; still, you couldn't tell, it was always worth trying.

You wanted her to come because with I-Mary there was al-ways a sense of something assured and comforting that you had expected and never found elsewhere . . . when you lay in the crib forlorn with that dreadful feeling which went by the name of "fever-nague," and you thought you would feel better if only Mama would take you up, as she did, and nothing happened! — when she sat down at twilight to rock the baby, and Jim leaned against her shoulder while she told stories about the war and old times, and you forgot and leaned against her knee until you felt it subtly withdrawing . . . "hadn't you better get your stool, Mary?" . . . So Mary sat on her little stool, Jim leaned against Mother's shoulder, and Jennie sat in her lap. But I-Mary suffered no need of being taken up and comforted; to be I-Mary was more solid and satisfying than to be Mary-by-herself [pp. 41–47].

Early in December, Mary was taken with a severe sore throat. It was one of those cases in which the doctor was not sent for because nobody knew what the trouble was. At night when her throat ached chokingly, Jennie would put her arms about Mary, stroking her face. So that after Mary recovered from her ailment, Jennie too came down with it. There was a little corner by the fire where she would sit, looking very ill, and trying patiently to respond to inquiry. There came a day when she could neither swallow nor speak. Aunt Effie came down that day and insisted that the doctor should be called, but it was then too late; probably in any case diphtheria was too little understood to have admitted of relief. The next day, in a belated recognition of the virulence of the disease, we buried her. I remember in the bleak little burying-ground looking up at my mother in her weeds and making toward her for the last time in my life the child's instinctive gesture for comfort, and being thrust off in so wild a renewal of Susie's own sense of loss, her rejection of what life had left for her, as leaves me still with no other comparison for the appalling

Mary Austin

shock and severance of widowhood. From that moment on the hillside under the leafless oaks above my father's grave, and my mother thrusting me away to throw herself upon it, I have no instant of recovered recollection until early the next spring when, as we were about to leave the farm to a tenant, the livestock and farming implements were put up for sale, which marks the end of the life on Plum Street.

In time I recovered from my father's death. For a long time I could recall so minutely how he looked that the sight of a man wearing a shawl — always he wore such a shawl as you may see in early portraits of Lincoln — was a fresh thrust in the wound. As late as 1908, walking London streets, I could pick out the resemblances of type, but doubt if I could recollect them now. Mary Patchen, when I met her, could recall to me little traits and mannerisms which else had gone clean out of my memory. But with Jennie it is not so. She is not changed or gone; nothing is changed, not the bright blue of her eye, the cherry lip, the soft aureole of her hair. Still in the night — such times as when I have written a book and see it for the first time in the cold obscenity of print and know without opening the pages that I have failed, that I have sold myself to the delusion of a task for which I have no endowment, an adventure unrequited — she comes in the first sleep and strokes my cheek with her soft hands. The loss of her is never cold in me, tears start freshly at the mere mention of her name. And I would not have it otherwise. She was the only one who ever unselfishly loved me. She is the only one who stays [pp. 86–87].

Earth Horizon

The road for which we had set out was El Camino Real, which is the King's Highway along which the towns of the Spanish foundation were strung from San Diego to San Francisco. The precise location of our journey's end was that district known as Tejon in the extreme southern end of the San Joaquin Valley, where there was still to be had Government land for the taking. But in spite of her anxiety to reach my brother, Mother was not proof against the Middlewestern obligation of visiting. We stopped over five days at Denver to see the Farrells, who were delighted to have us. Beyond the renewal of friendly interest, Mary recalls little of Denver except its impressive back-drop, and her disappointment that the city itself failed to differ markedly from other American cities she had seen. . . .

At Los Angeles, she was daunted by the wrack of the lately "busted" boom: the jerry-built bungalows, the blameless young palms abandoned along with the avenues they had been planted to adorn. The unwatered palms had a hurt but courageous look, as of young wives when they first suspect that their marriages may be turning out badly. One recoiled from the evidences of planlessness, the unimaginative economic greed, the idiot excitation of mere bigness, the strange shapeless ugliness, which, now that they were stripped of the leafage of boasting, was uncovered against the outraged loveliness of the coastal slopes. Mary was frightened; at least she was never more nearly frightened in her life; frightened of the commonplaceness of intention behind the exploded boom, the complete want of distinction in the human aspect of the country; frightened of the factitious effort of everybody to re-create a sense of the past out of sentiment for the Old Missions, out of *Ramona*, a second-rate romance very popular at the time, out of the miracle-mongering of overgrown vegetation and inflated prices. The few homes that she was admitted to were hodge-podges of cheap makeshift and tasteless newness, not entirely extenuated by the temporary character of residence. Mary began to ask herself, What have I come to? What if this thing should catch me? . . .

The Hunters were six or seven days on their hundred-mile journey, Mary on horseback, and the rest of the family by wagon, camping on the way. They went out past Eagle Rock, past low rounded hills on which the wild oats had dried moon-white and standing, patterned singularly with the dark cloudy green of live-oaks. They passed other boom towns, ambitiously laid-out plazas, partially surrounded by empty "business blocks," many of them stopped in mid-construction where the collapse of the boom had caught them; past acres of neglected orchard and vineyards being retaken by the wild. At San Fernando they turned out to visit the Mission, half-renovated to be the objective of tourist sight-seeing. Beyond that, old adobe ranch-houses with marks upon them of continuing Spanish occupancy began to appear, strings of chile drying on the outer walls, hides on the staked fences, chicken yards defended by prickly pear, old gnarled vines over the ramadas. We passed Camulus, the traditional home of "Ramona," the actual home of the Del Valle family. In San Fracisquito canyon at late afternoon, deer started from the ruddy thickets of manzanita; all along the hillsides tall fruiting stems of the yucca, called Candles of Our Lord, stood up. Between such points of interest, long stretches of the road, long since straightened for automobiles, rambled along the shallow dry beds of seasonal streams, called arroyos, dustily aromatic . . . rabbits and honored lizards scuttled there, road-runners perked and tilted, quail ran in droves.

There was something else there besides what you find in the books; a lurking, evasive Something, wistful, cruel, ardent; something that rustled and ran, that hung half-remotely, insistent on being noticed, fled from pursuit, and when you turned from it, leaped suddenly and fastened on your vitals. This is no mere figure of speech, but the true movement of experience. Then, and ever afterward, in the wide, dry washes and along the edge of the chaparral, Mary was beset with the need of being alone with this insistent experiential pang for which the wise Greeks had the clearest name concepts . . . fauns, satyrs, the ultimate Pan. Beauty-in-the-wild, yearning to be made human. Even in the first impact, Mary gave back a kindred yearning; it was in her mind that all she needed was to be alone with it for uninterrupted occasions, in which they might come to terms. And, as in this instance she was carried past the opportunity by the determination of her family to reach the San Joaquin Valley, so, later, the counter-obligations of a husband, a child, the necessity of earning a living, intervened.

The occasion for giving herself up wholly to the mystery of the arroyos never arrived. And meantime, the place of the mystery

Mary Austin

was eaten up, it was made into building lots, cannery sites; it re-ceded before the preëmptions of rock crushers and city dumps.

And still, whenever, out of a car window, over the wall of a rich man's garden, about which I am being proudly shown by the pro-prietor, I get sight of any not utterly ruined corner of it, I am torn in my vitals. This is the way a Naturist is taken with the land, with the spirit trying to be evoked out of it. This is the authentic note of confession for which autobiographies are supposed to be writ-ten, for which they are quite certainly read. It is time somebody gave a true report. All the public expects of the experience of practicing Naturists is the appearance, the habits, the incidents of the wild; when the Naturist reports upon himself, it is mis-taken for poetizing. I know something of what went on in Muir . . . for him, quite simply, the spirits of the wild were angels, who bore him on their wings through perilous places. But for Mary, the pietistic characteristics of the angels she had heard of pre-vented such identification. The human experience, which in the general mind could be most easily made to illustrate what she felt in the desert wild, was told her by a man she met years after, of the One Woman. He had met her when he was young and obsessed with the Life adventure. He knew her for what she was to be to him, and refused to know there were so many other charming women in the world; he didn't want to be taken with the net of permanence so early; he could come back to her when he had tried and preferred. And he was never able to get back. That was a long time ago, he said, and there were still times when he would be seized with the certainty of the One Woman, the dreadful, never-to-be appeased desire of her. . . . That was how it was with

Earth Horizon

Mary. She meant to come back to wrestle with the Spirit of the Arroyos, and she was never able. One quiet year to get a modern return on a persisting type of human experience on which even the intelligent Greeks spent themselves . . . not obtainable in the wealthiest country in the world!

Sometimes I think the frustration of that incomplete adventure is the source of the deep resentment I feel toward the totality of Southern California. It can't possibly be as inchoate and shallow as on its own showing it appears, all the uses of natural beauty slavered over with the impudicity of a purely material culture. Other times, away from it, I wake in the night convinced that there are still uncorrupted corners from which the Spirit of the Arroyos calls me, wistful with long refusals, and I resolve that next year, or the *next* at farthest . . . and I am never able to manage it.

That is what began to happen to Mary on the way up from Los Angeles to the Tejon that late summer of 1888. It took shape then as an intention; it seemed not difficult at all to come again, next summer, or the next. So, on the whole, that first trip made a very pleasant passage. At Gorman's, one of the oldest stage stations, we met Three-Fingered Bob, who told us that in Antelope Valley, which we passed through, the wind often blew so hard that it battered up the ends of crowbars. At Castac, under the oaks, a bear came down and frightened the horses, so that Mary and Jim had to take turns lying awake so that Susie might not be alarmed. Susie had taken timorously to sleeping out nights. The next afternoon they looked out from Tejon Pass on the vast dim valley.

Mary Austin

Mary wrote an account of that journey, a few weeks afterward, for her college journal, in which all the derived and imitative influence of academic training fell away, and she wrote for the first time directly, in her own character, very much as she did in *The Land of Little Rain*.

Three roads come into the oval curve of the San Joaquin Valley from the south. Toward the west the Temblor Road cut through the inner range to join El Camino Real, along which were strung the San Franciscan Missions; by this the sea and the low-lying coastal plain was reached. To the east the railroad came in, over Tehachapi Pass, touching Mohave where the desert wedged in, and connecting the central valleys with Los Angeles. Between the two, the Tejon road tapped the earliest settled districts and joined the Camino Real near San Fernando. At full length the road connected Los Angeles with San Francisco by way of the San Joaquin Valley towns, strung along the west-fronting slope of the Sierra Nevada, wherever a fruitful stream came down. The road's chief interest for the Tejon homesteaders was that it connected them with Bakersfield, the most southerly town, their source of supplies.

It was down this way Mary came, riding a buckskin horse, and watching as she came the road's white ambling beside the dark line, visible still from the heights, straightly drawn by the long-disused United States Mail Coach Line, and both of them disappearing into the vast dim hollow of the Valley, in the midst of which she could just make out the dark hieroglyphs of the Tulares. Off to the right, between barbed-wire fences, stretched the thirty thousand acres of Rancho El Tejon, and directly below it, outside the lower fence, in a narrow strip of waterless and there-fore unprofitable country, the half-dozen cabins of the home-steaders, in one of which she was now to make her home. There were no trees growing there, and no green grass, nor any shrubs taller than the sparse knee-high sagebrush; all tawny pale with summer heat. Pale cusps of treeless hills clipped the homestead-ers' strip on either side, and between it and the hollow of the Val-ley lay a low ridge of whitish, sandy dunes. Far on the eastern ho-rizon, above the heat haze, hung the long, snow-whitened slopes of the Sierra Nevada, from which the rivers came down to feed the vast tule swamps, whose intricate dark blurs were lost to sight as the travelers came down from the Pass.

I have forgotten, if ever I knew, why my brother came to fix upon this site for his homesteading venture, nor by what specious promises he had been led to suppose it even a fair gamble for suc-cess. There were not so many places where Government land could still be had under homesteader's filings, and like most of the then population of California, Jim was so newly come that he had as yet only a speaking acquaintance with the miracles of ir-rigation. Having seen these accomplished, newcomers were the readier prey for all manner of half-formulated and often rankly dishonest schemes for inducing their participation in irrigation canals that never were intended to be built, that never could have been built in the regions for which they were advertised. Perhaps for those who have it in their blood to "take up land" and expect to make a living out of it, no hazard seems too adventurous. In the case of my mother, there was the added inducement of having my father's service time deducted from the time requirement of

Mary Austin

"holding down a claim." We had a shack on hers and my brother's quarter-section; Mary's holding, being what was called a "timber claim," required no building.

There was something quaintly ancestral in our settling in; a one-room cabin, calico-curtained, bunks against the wall. The very names of our settler neighbors were familiar, Valentine, Morris, Stahl, Dunham, Adams, Johnson — tribe of congenital homesteaders. We combined on the necessary excursions to the waterhole, to the canyon for wood, to Bakersfield, thirty miles away across heavy sand, for mail and supplies.

For an age that counts distance on speedometers, one must reckon the trip to Bakersfield as between two and three hundred miles; two days of travel. Our neighbors usually started in the afternoon, camping on the way, but my mother never could quite bring herself to that; to camp out in the neighborhood of people like herself had for her the desolation of poverty. Fortunately, the Tejon Road had been not too remotely a stage-road, so that there were still respectable roadhouses at possible intervals. More than any other of the settlers, the Hunters sought the alleviations of the company store at Tejon Ranch, though the prices were high and the stock indifferent. The owner of the combined ranches of Tejon, La Liebre, and Castac had not lived on the property for years, but visited it occasionally from his home in Washington. The acting superintendent was an Englishman bred to the idea of landed estates, to whom the homesteaders outside the gates were no more than a slightly superior sort of gypsy. Nevertheless, we were all treated with reasonable courtesy. When the waters of

Earth Horizon

Grapevine Creek, which in good seasons spread far below the Tejon fence upon the plain, failed in the drought, we were allowed to go through the gates to a perennial waterhole under the cottonwood trees; and permits to hunt on Tejon property were not withheld. For the rest we all faithfully went through the motions of "making improvements" such as certified our intention to establish homes; heaping stones at the four corners of the land, plowing and planting where no seed could sprout, and by the prudent use of waste water coaxing a few cottonwood slips to grow.

As it turned out, we had come into the adventure at the worst possible juncture. The season of 1888 had been dry; 1889 was drier; 1890 proved the peak of desolation for an arid country. All that first winter rack-boned cattle tottered in the trails and died with their heads toward the stopped watercourses. The Tejon fences were cut and the cattle roamed where they could on Government land, cropping a few tindery mouthfuls. Since they could by no means keep the starved beasts from the unfenced homesteads, Tejon paid the settlers a nominal price for the nonexistent grass, which was the only income any of us ever had from our claims. In February when the settlers went through the perfunctory plowing and planting for the rains that did not come, pocket gophers and kangaroo rats walked in the powder-dry furrows and carried off grain after grain, as it fell, in their cheek pouches. That summer I recall it was necessary for the Tejon management to keep men and horses ready for dragging away the carcasses of the dead and dying cattle from unpleasant proximity to the settlers' water-barrels. It was the dreadful task of Mary and George to keep them from lying down in that vicinity; once down, they seldom got up again. For months the loma was all black with buzzards and the horrid announcing croak of them.

By the time the Hunters had settled in at Tejon, Mary suffered something like a complete collapse. There had been, in addition to the emotional stress of breaking up home, the two years of exhausting college work, in which so much of the other two years had to be made up by extra hours, after which had come the relaxing California climate, and the problem of food. I suppose few people who pioneered on the Pacific Coast between the Gold Rush in '49 and the Real Estate Rush in the eighties ever realized the natural food poverty of that opulent land. By that time the Spanish with the art of irrigation, and the Chinese, wise in food-growing, had mitigated the handicaps of an almost total want of native roots and fruits and nuts on which the Middlewest pioneers had managed mainly to subsist. It was only the few like the Tejon homesteaders, cast away on a waterless strip in a dry year, who realized that it had been the wiping away of the slowly accumulated Indian knowledge of native foods under the Franciscans, and the replacement of the wild herds with privately owned sheep and cattle, that made the tragedy of the forced abandonment of the Missions. For the settlers on the Tejon there was not so much as a mess of greens to be raised or gathered. It had all to be fetched from the town two days away, at prices that forced a cautious balancing between that and the still expensive and not very satisfactory canned fruits and vegetables. Strange now to recall that my mother never did become skillful in the utilization of canned foods, and that there persisted among housewives out of the self-sustaining rural households of the Middlewest an irreducible remainder of prejudice to their use.

During the first six months of homesteading, Mary suffered the genuine distress of malnutrition. There was no butter, and if anyone remembers what canned milk was like at that time, diluted with stale water from a dry-season waterhole — but I hope nobody does! For meat, we had game, plentiful if monotonous; rabbits, quail, and occasionally bear meat and venison bought from the "mountain men," grizzled derelicts of an earlier period, hidden away in tiny valleys, subsisting chiefly on the killing of venison and the robbing of bee trees. Mary, however, did not like game, especially rabbits, though she might have done better about it if she had not had to kill them. Mary was a fair shot, and with George to pick them up after they were killed, contrived to keep the family table reasonably supplied. Every little while the men of the neighborhood would go on a community hunt, especially in the winter months when there were ducks by thousands on the sloughs, and so we managed to live. My brothers, in fact, throve; George, who up till then had shown signs of being undersized and pudgy, began to shoot up and ended by being the tallest of the family. But Mary grew thinner and thinner, stooping under her weight of hair, and fell into a kind of torpor, of which undernourishment was probably the chief factor, a condition to which nobody paid any attention. Appetite, or the loss of it, was a purely personal matter. People guessed you would eat if you wanted it. What finally worried her mother was that Mary was unable to sleep. She would lie in her bunk with fixed, wide-open eyes, hearing the cu-owls on the roof, the nearly noiseless tread of coyotes going by in the dark, the strange ventriloquist noises they kept up with their cousins miles away beyond Rose Station, hearing the slow shuffling tread of the starved cattle, momentarily stopped by the faint smell of the settlers' water-barrels, but too feeble to turn out of their own tracks to come at them.

Nights when she and her mother slept at Susie's cabin, which was in a sandy wash, Mary would sit out among the dunes in the moonlight—Susie would never sleep there at any other times than full moon—watching the frisking forms of field mouse and kangaroo rat, the noiseless passage of the red fox and the flitting of the elf owls at their mating. By day she would follow a bobcat to its lair in the bank of the Wash, and, lying down before its den, the two would contemplate each other wordlessly for long times, in which Mary remained wholly unaware of what might happen to her should the wildcat at any moment make up its mind to resent her presence. There was a band of antelope on the Tejon range, fully protected by law, roving far down the hollow between the hills, passing between the wires of the fence as cleanly as winged things. There was a lone buck—the one who figures in the story of "The Last Antelope"—who tolerated her—it was not in his lifetime that the antelope had been accustomed to pursuit from men. Once in a storm of wind and rain they took shelter together in a half-ruined settler's shack. That was how Mary spent the first three months on the Tejon, all the time growing apparently more apathetic, until Susie was genuinely worried. "I can't help but think," she would say, "if you'd rouse yourself to take some interest in things . . ."

But the fact is Mary was consumed with interest as with enchantment. Her trouble was that the country failed to explain itself. If it had a history, nobody could recount it. Its creatures had no known life except such as she could discover by unremitting vigilance of observation; its plants no names that her Middle-western botany could supply. She did not know yet what were its weather signs, nor what the procession of its days might bring forth. Until these things elucidated themselves factually, Mary was spellbound in an effort not to miss any animal behavior, any bird-marking, any weather signal, any signature of tree or flower. Animals are like that, thrust into strange captivity, caught up into fearful question, refusing food and sleep until they die. But in Mary's case there was no fear but that she might miss the significance of the question, to which as yet she had no answer, the magic words which would unlock as much at least as anybody knew of the meaning of what she saw. For Mary is one of those people plagued with an anxiety to know. Other people, satisfied by the mere delight of seeing, think they pay her a compliment when they speak of her "intuition" about things of the wild, or that they let her down a deserved notch or two by referring to her fortunate guesses.

The deadlock was broken by the discovery, after the leaves were off, of wild grapes in one of the Tejon canyons, and after a week or two of almost exclusive grape diet, Mary began to pick up amazingly. It was so *like* Mary, her family remarked, to almost starve to death on a proper Christian diet and go and get well on something grubbed out of the woods. But there was more to the incident than that; there was the beginning of a notion in Mary's mind of a poor appetite of any sort being cured by its proper food; that there was something you could do about unsatisfactory conditions besides being heroic or a martyr to them, something more satisfactory than enduring or complaining, and that was getting out to hunt for the remedy. This, for young ladies in the eighteen-eighties, was a revolutionary discovery to have made. So that it appeared in the nature of a happy accident that General Edward Fitzgerald Beale, the owner of Tejon Ranch, came back to it along in January, 1889, and released Mary from the black spell of her wanting to know [pp. 181, 186–95].

Owens Valley, the precise point in it to which the Austins were bound, lies directly east of the southern San Joaquin, as the crow flies, but between them rose the Sierra Nevada in that notable cluster of peaks amid which the great rivers, Kearn, Kings, and Tuolumne, take their rise. The way into it from San Francisco was by way of Reno and a hesitant narrow-gauge railroad meandering down the Nevada, the snowy slope of the Sierra Range, to a long narrow trough of the earthquake drop that makes the great Sierra Fault, through which a river burrows to a bitter lake, cupped round with desertness. The road ends at Keeler on the shore of the lake, a bare huddle of houses beside the leprous-looking crusts of a vague business of commercial salts and borax-making, and an intermittent bottling of the waters from a hypothetical Castilian Spring of supposedly medicinal properties and unimaginable taste. The lake had been larger once, when the seasonal runoff of the mountain rains had been fuller, and was now so shrunk within its salty banks that nothing could grow near it but grayish salt bush and the arsenical green pickleweed. It lay there so thick with mineral residue that it was said no swimmer could sink in it, blankly opaque like a vast lidless eye, and gave always a portentous look to that end of Owens Valley. East and south there were low, treeless, mottled ranges beyond which was Death Valley, endless sun and silence. West and northward rose the stark wall of the Sierra Fault, and behind it thick ranks of peaks blotched dark with pines and white with snow, between which snow waters leaped and shouted to the thin line of towns to reach which one left the railroad and crossed the sunken river to within a mile or two of the canyons where the waters came through.

There were five of those towns, with several rural communities between, strung along the foot of the Sierra Wall, and it was to Lone Pine, the most southerly of these, that the Austins were bound. The irrigation ditch, the construction of which Wallace was to manage, had been taken out of the river in that vicinity; an earlier project which had been dropped for want of funds, which Frank was now supposed to have found. It was thought to be not only feasible, but promising immense returns through land opened up by it to settlement. That was all, absolutely all that Mary ever knew of the business that had brought her to that country. It was not expected of a young wife that she should in-

quire too closely into her husband's affairs. Mary's business, so
far as the physical distress of her condition allowed, was to sit under the huge cloudy cottonwoods that hung above the Lone Pine
Hotel and take in the strange wild beauty of the scene, and the
quaint, whimsical quality of the life there. Abruptly on the west
rose the vast ghost-gray bulk of Opopago, and behind it Whitney
towering to look down on Death Valley and west away to the rim
of the Pacific. Nothing saved the town from the sense of immi-
nent disaster from that overhanging bulk but the backs of an ancient line of treeless hills called Alabama, that ran along from the
lake's head a matter of a dozen miles or so to the north. On the
east rose the Opalescent Range that fenced the valley from pure
desertness, called Inyo, the name of the country, an Indian name
of which no one knew the meaning.

　You can read all this and more in *The Land of Little Rain*, or
you can reach the land itself by motor bus from Los Angeles in a
few hours. But on the life there, the unforgettable life, modern
America has laid a greedy, vulgarizing hand. When Mary was
first there, life stood at the breathing pause between the old ways
and the new. In Death Valley wheel tracks lay undisturbed in the
sand where the unhappy Jayhawkers had passed in '49, and
marks of the tent-pegs where Booth played "Julius Cæsar" in the
great days of the Comstock, faintly tracked the ground. There
were people who remembered these things. Others recalled
when the Paiutes in their last stand were driven into the bitter
waters of the lake, and dying, sunk there. There were Indians
who had stories to tell of the last great struggle between Paiutes
and the Southern Shoshones and of the gathering-up of the clans

when Beale became Indian Commissioner and removed them to Tejon. Older and older there was myth and legend, and all up and down that country the pictoglyphs that marked the passage of ancient migrations, and strange outline ruins of forgotten villages in the black rock country which must have been made when the rains fell plentifully and game roamed over regions where now not so much as a wind stirred.

During the latter days of the Comstock era, mining enterprise had spread all down the inner ranges, as far as Coso and Panamint, and was still going on there feebly. Towns had sprung up in Owens Valley where food could be raised, and men kept their families while they ransacked the waterless hills. With the slow decline of mining, agricultural possibilities in Inyo began to come to the fore, until the sudden enlargement during the past decade of irrigation and fruit-growing in Southern California had drawn off both interest and capital to the more accessible lands, and there, between the old era and the new, the Valley hung, so that if Frank Austin's ditch company had succeeded, something of the same thing that was happening elsewhere might have happened here in the shadow of the Sierras between the highest point of American land and the lowest. But the district about Lone Pine was still full of myth and factual reminder of lucky strikes, stage-coaches, bandits, and Indian uprisings. Mary sat contentedly under the cottonwoods for a few weeks absorbing these things.

Then one day her husband disappeared soon after breakfast, and Mary, coming back from her daily walk, found her trunk out on the sidewalk and her room closed. She sat on her trunk in the

sun and looked anxiously up and down the road. She felt that the
landlady had taken an unfair advantage to bring matters to this
pass while her husband was away. She sat on the trunk for hours,
all her energies concentrated on not breaking down. About four
o'clock a woman she knew came by and suggested that there was
a boarding-house on the far edge of town where she might find
accommodation. It proved a longish walk to the farmhouse which
was now a place where miners, touched with the lead poisoning
common to the local ores, recuperated under a diet of milk and
fruit. Mrs. Dodge, the landlady, was having a Kaffee Klatch all
by herself. She offered Mary a piece of coffee cake along with the
information that her feet hurt, that her cook had left her, and that
too many of her boarders were dilatory about paying their board.
Mrs. Dodge was an ample, toilworn German woman, speaking
English very badly, rough of tongue, but kind of heart. When
Mary revealed who she was and what she wanted, Mrs. Dodge
did her best to steel herself to remember only that she was a landlady. She wouldn't be taking any more boarders. The way she was
situated she ought to be out in the kitchen this minute making
pies, but with her feet hurting the way they did, she didn't see
how in hell — besides, everybody was saying that the ditch
people weren't paying their bills — but she had revealed too
much. "Oh, well," said Mary, "I'll make the pies."

The pies turned out beautifully, and Mrs. Dodge, appeased,
agreed to let Mary stay and help with the cooking for her room
and board. At supper Mary had a good look at the other boarders, and on the surface of her mind considered that she might be
entertained by the situation. Deep within her there was a place

where humiliation and anxiety should have been, which was dull and stonied. About dusk her husband came — he had been to the hotel and someone had told him where to find her — and she realized that he had been all day without food and had no money to buy it. She began automatically to do the things a young wife will do when her man comes home at night and she must feed him. You should have seen the imperturbable ladyhood with which the newly acquired cook at Dodge's overrode the German woman's sense of imposition. Did I say somewhere that Mary was an actress — in the bone? David Belasco, who saw her once when she was at it, said, "Oh, lady, if you had come to me twenty years ago!" Mary was too polite to tell him that twenty years ago she had not heard of him. You would have thought the case-hardened landlady would have done herself an injury through suppressed indignation as Mary set out the remains of the supper without so much as leave asked. "You don't look like you was goin' to be able to earn your board and his'n," remarked Mrs. Dodge significantly. But fortunately Mary remembered that at a pinch she could sew; she could even cut and fit [pp. 233–36].

Mary contrived to get back to her mother in September. That night Susie came to her bedside and kissed her . . . in accordance with Susie's Scotch bringing-up, the Hunters kissed only for the formal occasions of greeting and parting. Mary could have wept over this one voluntary caress she had to remember, except for the necessity she felt for not letting her mother know what other reasons she had for crying. Mary's daughter was born October 30, and called Ruth, as the only name that had not yet been sponsored or opposed by some member of the family. The interest that her brothers took in their new niece was the one spontaneous relief to an occasion the memory of which is like some poor prisoner's of the wheel and the rack.

I know now, of course, that Mary was not physically constituted for child-bearing, and that the medical care accessible was not even the best for the time; the merely acceptable rural practice, not untouched with the superstitions of my mother's generation. The doctor was called away in the midst of it for four hours, to cut off a man's leg, hurt in a well-boring accident. On the ninth day, said her mother, any woman with any pride in herself must get up. Mary did as she was told; the next day the doctor had to be sent for, and months of shattering, debilitating consequences ensued.

There was worse. Mary had come to the end of her own resources for warning or acting. Since the failure of the ditch company, Wallace had earned not more than a few dollars. Mary was not only dependent on her family in every particular, but before she was out of bed with her confinement, there broke around her the realization that everything relating to her marriage had been done, as it was easy to do at that time, on a credit basis, and that there were debts going back of the marriage and involving practically every event of the last two years. Wallace, who had established himself at a mountain camp with one friend he had made in Inyo, on what terms Mary was afraid to ask, could not be easily got at. He wrote to her to do what she thought best about things and let it go at that. The Hunters were not people who went in debt. It was probably the expectation of "getting it out of the family" that brought her husband's creditors down upon her at this time. Jim was at first disposed to undertake adjudication of the mess, but was put out, naturally, by Wallace's failure to make any contributive admissions or statement of his affairs. If at this time Mary had chosen to put herself entirely in their hands, her family would have taken her back, and against all their moral prejudices have agreed to a divorce. But Mary was not yet prepared for that. She had to face, as the family was still unable to realize, their incomprehensible want of sympathy with her way of life and the total surrender of her right to it that would have been involved in such a concession.

She still believed in the solution of the personal problem by the application of intelligence. The surprises of the past two years had been disconcerting, and the obligations of her condition had prevented their being forcefully met. But she thought that if she could only talk things over with her husband — She knew now that he knew, that day he left her alone at the hotel, what was to happen. And Mrs. Dodge had told her that it happened when it did because the community had offered him the principalship of the school a few days before and he had refused it. This was difficult to understand, but Mary felt confident that there was an explanation. She would go to her husband and they would talk it out and come to an understanding and begin all over again. There was nothing two intelligent people couldn't do together if they set about it.

While Mary was still in bed, the first of her stories was published in the *Overland*. Susie read it aloud to her, but she could never be got to express an interest in it. "I think you could have made more of it," Mary finally dragged out of her. Where was now the triumph and encouragement that should go to one's first professional adventure! The *Overland* paid, on publication, three dollars a page if I remember. Mary sent it secretly to her husband for a Christmas present, and that was that.

Early in the spring, Wallace was elected to fill out the term at one of the district schools, which the teacher had just abandoned in order to marry. On that assurance of food and shelter, as soon as the weather would permit, Mary packed her baby in a market-basket and set out by rail and stage-coach for Inyo. She was then something less than twenty-three and had not sat up for the whole of any day since her confinement [pp. 238–40].

The journey I took before writing "The Land of Journey's Ending" did more for me than simply to gather up the detailed presentment of the Southwest. It gathered all the years of my life, all my experience; my intentions; it determined the years that were left. California had slipped away from me. Sterling's death and other changes at Carmel had made of it a faded leaf, pressed for remembrance. New York had failed to engage the exigent interests of my time. It was not simple nor direct enough; bemused by its own complexity, it missed the open order of the country west of the Alleghenies. It was too much intrigued with its own reactions, took, in the general scene, too narrow a sweep.

Earth Horizon

It lacked freshness, air and light. More than anything else it lacked pattern, and I had a pattern-hungry mind. I liked the feel of roots, of ordered growth and progression, continuity, all of which I found in the Southwest. Although I knew that I was probably putting much of my audience behind me, I knew that in electing to live there I was releasing myself to a larger scope. I knew that my work, which was essentially of the West, like "The Land of Little Rain," "The Flock," and "The Land of Journey's Ending," had a permanent hold on the future. It could not be overwritten nor left to one side. After I came back from that journey, I began explicitly to put New York behind me. . . .

There was a curious light thrown upon this problem of the essential relationships of men and women by a set of experiences initiated soon after my arrival in New York, and continued at intervals throughout my stay there. It began with an effort to know New York, the face of it, what went on in its streets and neighborhoods, its hours and occasions. As soon as my day's stint of writing was done, I would be out, going up one street and down another, observing, inquiring, and checking, and, where I found special quarters of interest, arranging to stay in them for days, even for weeks, in whatever character would get me closest to the quality of the life there. Sometimes I simply rented rooms in the character of a typist; other times I sought employment and made myself part of the working community. What I was looking for was the web of city life, the cross-ties and interweavings which brought all classes into coalition, made the city unit. It was one of the complaints of my life there that it was too limited, kept within a narrowly circumscribed social round, so that with the immense mass of city dwellers I had no manner of contact. I had it in mind, of course, that I would make fiction of my findings, fiction which would do what nobody was doing in fiction for New York, presenting a closely woven section of the life of the city. As a matter of fact, I never found it. There were cities; whorls of social contact and activity which went on within themselves apart and aside from all other manifestations, except as they were deliberately sought out as I was seeking them. I went down into the Cherry Street district and plied my typewriting trade, completely alienated from every other contact. I stopped in the neighborhood south and east of Washington Square and worked at artificial flowers. I went "partners" with a peddler of shoelaces and pencils. Over on the west side below Forty-Second Street, I boarded at a place which catered to railroad employees, and picked up a "steady" of the Brotherhood of Railway Engineers. I sublet two rooms in the Chelsea district, from a woman who told me her husband was "in the law business; at the City Hall, you know." It turned out that he was a hanger-on of the city courts, an "alibi" man, who, when an alibi or a witness was wanted, engaged to produce him. He was a friendly soul. I was ill with flu while there, and he used to bring me a comforting brown bottle and sit by my bed and tell me incidents of his practice. In the same house was a couple who had three sons in the police, who came home once or twice a week to play a game of pinochle with their old man and have a taste of mother's cooking, to which I was occasionally invited. In another place I made the acquaintance of a stranger from Chicago, an expert in cement foundations for skyscrapers, who taught me more about the city that is under the city than I could have imagined, the trend of the rocks, the underground waters. He was a clean and sober Irish-American, one who had fathered his widowed mother's brood and brought them to successful issues, and was now at forty-two alone and at loose ends. We went to the pictures together, and to a "show," which was all he knew of the drama, and to concerts in the social hall of Saint Patrick's Parish. And finally he began to tell me how cheaply one could live in Chicago, and about the butchers' picnic and the Sunday lakeside excursions, so that it became necessary for me to behave like a gentleman and — having on that occasion represented myself as a newspaper woman — get sent out of town, leaving no address behind. I worked under the Elevated at a hairshop, which specialized in dressmakers' show window dummies. The keeper of the shop was a middle-aged German Jewish woman, plain and harsh to everyone but her husband, younger than herself, a hunchback, and an artist in his trade. He used to go to the Opera House and to the streets of fashionable weddings to observe the hairdressing of the fine ladies, which he repeated in his dummies, working at them with an artist's concentration. He chose to make me the confidante of his raptures, so that his wife became aware of it, and I lost my job. For that was the one single item which held throughout the whole range of these experiences, that the men accepted me at face-value, they never found me out, never so much as suspected me of a life of my own apart from what I showed. Sometimes the women were suspicious; the mother of my policemen friends, the wife of my alibi man. But no man ever discovered in me anything but the attraction of strangeness, the flattery of interested attention. My cement foundation worker never so much as inquired which paper I worked upon, nor did my Brotherhood engineer question my complete satisfaction with the scope and outlook of what he had to offer; so that it comes over me, when I think of the men who with more reason might have expected to mate successfully with me, that the failures grew out of an essentially male incapacity to realize what other factors than reciprocal passion entered into such mating. There were none of them able to make room for me, as a person, however much as a woman I might be desired; and on my part, love was not enough.

It was with the realization, however, of the limitations of experience that I settled in my mind that I would write the closing years of my life into the history of Santa Fé. I could be useful here; and I felt I could get back a consideration from the public that would in a measure make up for the loss of certified ladyhood. I do, in a measure, get taken care of here; I call on the community for help and coöperation — from the doctor, the lawyer, the banker, the artist, the business man — and the response is prompt and sure. It was an intuitive feeling for the reality of such response that led me, shortly after my return from the long journey, to purchase a plot of ground at the foot of Cinco Pintores Hill and later to build upon it.

Once having determined upon Santa Fé as my future home, I never quite let go of it. I returned from time to time; especially I visited Mabel and Tony Luhan at Taos. By this time they had brought their several affairs to the conclusion of marriage and a satisfactory social adjustment. Mabel had built a spacious house on the edge of the Pueblo allotment, and half a dozen guest-

Earth Horizon

houses on the adjoining field, where one met people of interest and distinction. One meets there people like Robert Edmond Jones, a great favorite of mine, and Robinson Jeffers, D. H. Lawrence, Georgia O'Keeffe, Agnes Pelton, Carlos Chavez. I went there often, for while there is practically no likeness between Mabel and me, very little consenting approval, there is the groundwork of an intelligent approach to problems of reality, and a genuine affection. There is about Tony a warm stability of temperament which makes him an acceptable third to all our intercourse, so that I count among the unforgettable experiences of New Mexico the journeys we have taken, journeys of exploration and recollection, laying ourselves open to the beauty, the mystery, and charm of New Mexico. Tony is an exceptionally good driver, not like the average American driver who constitutes himself merely the master of the car's mechanisms, the exhibitionist, but making it the extension of his personality. Tony puts the car on, and when he begins, as he does usually, to sing the accentless melodies of his people which fit so perfectly to the unaccented rhythms of the machine, one has the sensation of sailing on the magic carpet along the floor of space. Time brings us all closer in these things, so that my life here is extended, practically and emotionally, by the inclusion of Mabel and Tony and the house at Taos [pp. 349, 351–55].

I had let the contract for my house and was in the worst possible situation to endure a serious illness such as, on consultation, mine proved to be, and the decision that I must have an operation

Mary Austin

. . . from which I was a year in recovering. What I discovered was that not only had I been obliged to give up my commissions, but the manuscript of the novel which I had half-completed was missing. In the confusion of my illness and moving, it had been lost.

I do not know how I should have survived all this illness and disaster had it not been for that kindness and care which I had intuitively anticipated among my friends at Santa Fé. Particularly the Applegates. They were an Illinois family of old kin and kindness, and my nearest neighbors. Frank was an artist, and equally interested with me in the Spanish colonial arts and crafts. Alta reminded me of my sister Jennie, in appearance and in the quality of lovableness. She played a sister's part to me. By means of these things I began to regain my health. . . .

About that time Frank Applegate and I had gone so far with the Spanish colonial arts that it seemed worth while to attempt their revival. I did not know that I should live to see the enterprise through, but I thought that if I had to leave it, somebody would be raised up to carry it on. Also I knew that if I could make a tolerable beginning, I should increase my own chances of living. I knew by this time that what had seen me thus far was the persistent character of my progressive activity. If something in me went on, I would go on with it. I got up from my bed and set the revival of the Spanish colonial arts in motion.

New Mexico is a bilingual country; the courts, the legislature, most public worship, is conducted in two languages. And in two languages everything made is expressed. The colonists who came here originally came direct from Spain; they had not much tarrying in Mexico. They brought with them what they remembered, and as soon as they began to create, they made things in the likeness of the things of old Spain, modified by what they found here among the Indians. For the first hundred years they made very little; they were simply being conditioned by what they found. They accepted the Indian house, but added a fireplace; they brought chests, but added tables and chairs in the Spanish pattern. They made *santos* and *bultos* in the pattern of the holy images of sixteenth-century Spain. When they began to weave, it was in the pattern of Southern stuffs with a little suggestion from Mexico. They mixed with the Indians, the peon class, and brought into their blood an Indian strain, Indian capacity for making things, for design and color. These things had been beautiful, but the hundred years of American influence had broken them down and they had not learned to make much else. It takes more than a hundred years to destroy patterns in the blood.

Frank began to collect the old things, to sort them and put values on them. He bought an old house and began to restore it; he collected *santos* and old furniture and tin work. By this time I had begun to collect the folk literature, the plays, the legends and songs. . . . We began a permanent collection of native arts; I collected scores of native plays and *corridos* and songs. There was, a little north of Santa Fé, an excellent example of an old private chapel, with painted reredos and altar and decorations. The family who owned it was dwindling and finally decided to sell it, made terms with a curio dealer. I was away from home when this happened, at Yale. Frank wired me, and I managed to raise the money to buy it in, to keep it for a religious memorial.

Mary Austin

That was after Willa Cather came to write *Death Comes for the Archbishop*, and I had to go to the hospital. Miss Cather used my house to write in, but she did not tell me what she was doing. When it was finished, I was very much distressed to find that she had given her allegiance to the French blood of the Archbishop; she had sympathized with his desire to build a French cathedral in a Spanish town. It was a calamity to the local culture. We have never got over it. It dropped the local mystery plays almost out of use, and many other far-derived Spanish customs. It was in the rebuilding of that shattered culture that the Society for the Revival of the Spanish Arts was concerned [pp. 356–59].

The Land of
Journeys' Ending

*M*ary Austin's return to and travels in the Southwest underlie The Land of Journeys' Ending. *Her longtime friendship and correspondence with the eminent botanist Dr. Daniel T. MacDougal of the Carnegie Institute of Washington and the University of Arizona furnished much of the book's material and reveals the level of Austin's scientific understanding;* The Land of Journeys' Ending *is dedicated to him. Published in 1924, it is a companion to* The Land of Little Rain, *a rounding out, a life brought full circle. Both books deal with the desert landscape, observed with clarity, researched with diligence, and in both there are strong passages of deeply felt writing.* The Land of Little Rain *is a first book,* The Land of Journeys' Ending *a mature work, showing Austin's powers of observation sharpened with time, the sweep of her writing both expansive and precise. The book plan is simple. There are chapters on history and on different venues of the Southwest, much of which was unfamiliar or more likely unknown to most readers at the time. Familiar as the Southwest is now, seventy years later, today's reader must realize that the research she did was new. To understand this is to appreciate the intelligence of her writing, the generosity of her research, and the value of this early, coherent, thoughtful look at the Southwest.*

The last short selection, on Inscription Rock, sums up Austin's identification with nature, her embuing of place with human spirit, a sense of oneness with the desert that in the end was both Austin's salvation and the attribute that invigorates all her writing about the desert. As she walked a terrain Coronado knew four centuries earlier, she portrayed a desert landscape glowing with light and health.

Mary Austin

Between the Rio Colorado and the upper course of the Rio Grande lies the Land of Journeys' Ending.

No such natural boundaries, but the limits of habitableness, define it north and south. About the sources of its inclosing rivers the ranges of the continental axis draw to a head in the Colorado Rockies. Southward they scatter, like travelers who have lost their heads in terror of desertness, among the vast unwatered plateaus of Old Mexico. But all the country east of the Grand Cañon, west and north of the Jornada del Muerto, is like the middle life of a strong man, splendidly ordered. This is the first sense of the land striking home to the traveler who gives himself up to it. Go far enough on any of its trails, and you begin to see how the world was made. In such a manner mountains are thrust up; there stands the cone from which this river of black rock was cast out; around this moon-colored *playa*, rises the rim of its ancient lake; by this earthquake rent, the torrent was led that drained it. What man in some measure understands, he is no longer afraid of; the next step is mastery.

That this is the first and the lasting effect of the country comprised in the western half of New Mexico and the whole of Arizona, may be discovered, if from no other source, from the faces of the men who first made it habitable. In any collection of pioneer portraits you will find one type of physiognomy predominating—full-browed, wide between the eyes, and, in spite of the fierce mustachios and long curls of the period, with a look of mildness. Superior to the immediate fear of great space, of the lack of water or the raiding savage, there was a subtle content at work. Seeing ever so short a way into the method of the land's making, men became reconciled to its nature.

There can be no adequate discussion of a country, any more than there can be of a woman, which leaves out this inexplicable effect produced by it on the people who live there. To say that the Southwest has had a significant past, and will have a magnificent future, because it is a superb wealth-breeder, is to miss the fact that several generations of men wasted themselves upon it happily, without taking any measure of its vast material resources. The nineteenth-century assault which found California a lady of comparatively easy virtue, quailed before the austere virginity of Arizona; but the better men among them served her without recompense. If the Southwest is becoming known as an unrivaled food-producer, still, food-producing is one of the things man has taught the land to do since has has lived in it. There was nothing that betrayed its crop capacity to the untutored sense of the Amerind savage and the unlettered American pioneer. Both of these married the land because they loved it, and afterward made it bear. If more lines of natural development converged here, between the bracketing rivers, more streams of human energy came to rest than anywhere else within what is now the United States, it was because men felt here the nameless content of the creative spirit in the presence of its proper instrument.

Such a country as this, calls its own from the four world quarters. It had called many known and some forgotten peoples before any European, just to hear of it, had been afoot, in that neighborhood, and that not of his own wish, for seven years [pp. 3–5].

At the turn of the two seasons, following the march of the sun home from the north or up from the south, a far-flung wing of storm sifts fine snow like down, or finer rain, over the masked shapes that by a solemn movement of their boughs give thanks. In May or April, in the storm-cleared space that no seedling has yet preëmpted for its own, white borage or blue nemophila creeps low as a church mouse, and the black-and-white flash of a magpie's wings startles like the striking of a match. Nothing else for a thousand years.

East of the Rio Grande the junipers are small and widely interspersed among the green rosettes of the one-leaved piñon pines, with which the pale hills are spotted like an ocelot. The green of the junipers is slightly yellower than the pines, which may also be identified for the stranger by their tendency to run to a true tree form with an upright stem, and by the blue back and the white ellipse of the spread wings of the piñonero, the piñon jay, whose winter pasturage is extracted from small, globose cones. From Raton Pass, the gateway of New Mexico, juniper and piñon hold steadily south and west until they give place, beyond Albuquerque, to mesquite and creosote and saltbush, each keeping to its kind, in open order on a gravelly, grassless ground.

The Land of Journeys' Ending

It is this prevalence of a single type of growth over enormous areas, combined with the lack of surface cover for the naked, fire-colored sands, that gives the Southwest its undeserved reputation for desertness. To most people a forest is a persisting communality of tree and plant life, thought of in collective terms as one thinks of a city. What you have here is a pine and another pine and another, mesquite and mesquite and mesquite, each in its inviolate circle of bare earth, bound together by not so much as the roots of grass. And to many people grass is as indispensable an index of fertility in the earth as long hair is of femininity in a woman. Actually, all that grass and other annual cover afford to the casual observer, is evidence of the quick, continuous rhythms of vegetating life. But in arid regions where the period of growth is confined to the short season of maximum rainfall, the processes of foliation and floration are pushed almost to explosion; followed by a long quiescence in which life merely persists. To feel the growing pulse of the New Mexican forest, you must take to the trail weeks before the high passes are open, loitering about the Santa Fé highlands until you discover, in the leaning towers of the yellow pine along the lowest limit of summer waters, the magpie on whose wings are the footsteps of the morning. If you see one, cross yourself and return to your home. But two together are a fortunate omen.

The first sound of spring in the Rio Grande country is the sound of snow-water. In the March-April Moon, the Moon of the Rabbit Brush Disappearing, when the Indians take down their windbreaks and shelters, snow may still fall. Lodging like fluffs of cloud on the flat roofs and the finely divided foliage of the piñon pines, it begins at once to sparkle with the dew of the drip. The drip quickens to a gurgle. Pools, yellow but mirror-bright, collect in the hollows of the road, so that your car seems every moment about to plunge into an abyss of basalt cliff and cambric sky. Lacy hummocks on the sage and the cedars are undercut by the warm breath of the earth, and the trickle of snow-water is intermittent with the swish of dropping wreaths and straightening boughs.

By this time the rabbit-brush has lost its veil of winter fluff; its pale stalks, passing insensibly into light along the banks of washes, are defined only by the green smudge at the base of its dry fascicles. Bluebirds flutter in the chaparral like flecks of falling sky; the willows are lacquered orange and vermilion. Now the wind has a growing smell, but along the wooded tops of the ranges snow still filters delicately through the rarefied air. The diffused, shut-in light of the snow is like the whiteness of rapid vibration, the earth envelop disappearing in a mist of its own motion. Farther south, where snow is made rain midway of the vault, the storm, seen moving across the *abras* from the inclosing hills, has the effect of emanating from the ground, as if the earth exhaled it, and, by a gentle, down-streaking motion, drew it to its breast again.

Between the last snows and the coming of the green, broken-winged cold winds play between the ranges. The dried water-courses are picked out by lifting veils of dust as the wind struggles woundedly with the returning sun. Around the Little Colorado, which was once called Rio de Lino because of the flax that

The Land of Journeys' Ending

grew there, and on the *plan del Zuñi* and all sandy washes toward the west, there is a Bigelovïa which at this season gathers a silvery lint along stems that are milky blue with the cold, and on a day are suddenly, definitely green. About this time, walking among the junipers, still sticky yellow and friable like discarded Christmas trimmings, first one and then another pricks itself on your attention. As if all the vitality of the tree, which during the winter had been withdrawn to the seat of the life processes underground, had run up and shouted, "Here I am." Not one of all the ways by which a tree strikes freshly on your observation, — with a greener flush, with stiffened needles, or slight alterations of the axis of the growing shoots, accounts for this flash of mutual awareness. You walk a stranger in a vegetating world; then with an inward click the shutter of some profounder level of consciousness uncloses and admits you to sentience of the mounting sap.

But it is only in the low growths of the New Mexico highlands, where, as you walk, your head comes level with the forest crown, that it happens with authority. What can we know of trees whose processes of elongation toward the light go on a hundred feet or more overhead? Only occasionally, after a long time in the tall forest, doing nothing and thinking very little, a sense of the alien and deeply preoccupied life of the tree shakes our less experienced human consciousness with a touch called Panic.

There is an exceeding subtlety about the spring in New Mexico, at once virginal and experienced, like Mona Lisa's smile. The planted orchards hold aloof, the wild-plum thickets are tiptoe for flight. Suddenly at the end of May, from painted-cup and filmy cactus-flower blazons forth the secret of that country, the secret of fire that gave it birth.

Farther south, where there is more sun and all the rain is drunk by the sand, there is a briefer and more varied bloom, miles and miles of yellow poppies fluttering their cups an inch or two from the powdery earth, whole hill-slopes streaked along the stream-lines with nearly stemless, pale-gold cruciferæ. Later, two or three varieties of yucca and agave send up tall banners of whitish bloom in companies like marching men.

But across the Santa Fé highlands and the tall potreros of the Rio Grande, the local growth takes color of the dark conifers against the rose and ocher clays, black trap and dazzling pumice. Where the scant soil on the flat tops of the potreros thins out the conifers, blood-red flowers of nopál open delicately to the light, and from tuft to tuft of bunch-grass the young winds stalk one another [pp. 36–41].

The aspen itself is the peculiar treasure of the upper water-courses; sparsely branched, delicately leaved, a lady tree, a fairy-lady tree forever ruffling her petticoats or washing her gold hair beside the dark duenna pines. High up, circling a mountain meadow, its white-limbed branchlets flow each to the other like Botticelli's nymphs. Thick ranked along the water-borders of the Rio Grande as it comes through the Culebra, the straight green-ish boles carrying their thyrses of shifty, pattering pale leaves fifty or sixty feet above the stream-bed, it becomes mysterious, formidable as massed femininity. All summer the leaves of the quaking aspen are pale glaucous green, but in the Moon of the Cold Touching Mildly, which is also the month of the sun turning south, they are coined anew of glinting gold, making gold of all the air. The cottonwoods, stayed all summer along the lower river-bottoms and around solitary water-holes, like green umbrageous clouds, burn suddenly hot gold. . . . I remember, over Galisteo way, where the walls of the houses are all rosy from the rosy earth, one that cast a spell on me, burning solitary, in the clear yellow of every perfect leaf, in the hollow of a turquoise sky!

In the northern pueblos at the feast of Poseyemo, which has been approximated to the day of that Christian saint whose festival comes nearest the autumnal equinox, the dancers hold their bright aspen boughs toward the rays of departing Poseyemo, the legend of whose journey south was very early assimilated to the sun-myth. But, in their ritual cosmogony, the aspen stands for the golden east from which, in the manner of all Great Ones, their Poseyemo is expected to return. Thus by way of its evergreenness, its goldness, by white blossom styles, by pollen clouds such as the blue larkspur sheds to be the fertility-invoking medicine of the Navajo bride's marriage basket, the plant world begins to stand to man not for itself but for ideas. And in this fashion begins the long process which leads from the thing to its idea, by way of its name and pictured shape, to the discovery of print. But few of *us* read the plant world as a book; by all our ways of speaking of it, denying the thing that happened. Even I, saying that the best bows are made of juniper wood! when, in fact, before there could be a bent stick from which a pointed stick could be launched, there was the idea of the bow arching in the bough of the juniper, making itself known to man by springy branches, being drawn down and flying back, catapulting light weights; bending, not breaking. By even more subtle ways of catching his attention, of which, after long uninterrupted hours with it, I have a hint, the juniper got itself made into bows. By such direct, dark paths, lost and only occasionally recovered, the wild grass and the tree on the mountain yearned toward and made themselves evident in man [pp. 45–46].

The choice of habitat among arid-region plants is governed by the nature of the adjustments they have learned to make to the restricted water-supply. In the country below the Rim there are three general types of adjustment, the first of which is the speeding up of the vegetating cycle of plants that elsewhere take the whole summer season for flower and fruit. Thus within a few days after the winter solstice, the borages begin to send up leafy spikes as thick as hairs, and within a few days have matured their white prickly burrs. Verbena flowers in the sand, and the decumbent Callindra cover the low hills with a delicate rosy fringe. Alfileria, a relative of our eastern cranes-bill, spreads in every available space its flat rosettes of lanceolate leaves and pinkish flowers, followed by the long-billed fruits that children stick in their stockings to tell them what o'clock it is.

Within the same few days, poisonous green plats of loco-weed widen along the washes, wither, and leave their pale, papery pods to rustle about the sand. But the very swiftness with which the reproductive cycle is accomplished, leaves the field of observation to be dominated by the second type of adjustment in which the life of the individual plant is infinitely prolonged, as in the creosote bush, which grows according to the rain, waits and grows and waits, for two or three hundred years, and with the flight of its delicate shadows on the swept sand makes an effect of motion without change or sound from which impressions of the country below the Rim are inseparable. Occupying the gravelly upper levels of the vast *abras*, the creosote is easily recognizable by its springy slender boughs, crowned with fine, sparse foliage, varnished until it gives back the light in a green sparkle.

After the winter solstice brings the first of the rains, the creosote covers itself with thin yellow corollas that detach themselves on the wind in flocks like butterflies, and within a week or two are followed by tiny cotton balls, bursting white and lining the runnels of the later rains with fluff. A little later, across the clayey *playas* the delicate feather-form foliage of the mesquite and the acacias blows under the green moons of summer twilights like green hair.

When the track of the sun behind the western ranges passes insensibly into bands of pale citron, half-way up the sky, which at this latitude holds on a deep liquid blue until midnight, the earth walks a virgin. From the tall peaks, one by one, the rosy light is let go like smiles she leaves behind her on the way to her devotions. Dark ranges fold about her as a cloak; there is no sound, nor any motion except the blowing of her hair.

Mary Austin

Of other desert shrubs and trees which contribute to the effect of delicacy in the landscape of southern Arizona, the most important is the palo-verde, lifting its sharply etched, leafless brooms well above the mesquite, outlining the dry washes. In Papagueria, and south into Sonora, the palo-verde becomes a veritable tree, "big bean tree," and in wet years its bright-green stems put forth minute scale-like leaves that vanish with the rains. In May or June, between its wire-like twigs are caught swarms of delicate flowers of that lovely, lively color that painters call king's yellow, lining the streamways like the stroke of a loaded brush across the landscape. Long after nightfall the palo-verde may be located by its honey-locust scent, carried by little fitful airs that play about the bolsons after the sun goes down, left in the warm hollows like a dropped handkerchief.

In that long dry wash which runs parallel to the Santa Fé railroad just east of the crossing of the Colorado, both the mesquite and the creosote may be observed, growing apart in the white dust, also the palo-verde, and that other fine-haired desert shrub, the Arizona smoke-bush, disappearing into a mist of its own infinitely divided tips. Here, at the edge of the streamways, is Findler's rose, its furzy green starred with small, white, yellow-hearted bloom, between the dense, dusty globes of *garamboya*.

Farthest from the crossing where the wash begins, there is a plantation of shaggy tree yuccas, the Joshua-tree of the plainsman, and clusters of dead-looking long wands close-bundled at the root, which in May or June may be recognized by their scarlet tips, as ocotillo. This is the only locality with which I am familiar in which so many of the types of arid growth may be found together. In the great *abras* farther inland, they occupy uninterrupted miles of their chosen levels, with scarcely any other company. Even grass, if it grows at all in this country, prefers the company of grass. High on the bajadas, slopes too steep to hold the soil that even the humbler sort of shrubs demand, or masking lava flows not yet worn down to nourishing dust, great patches of *Hillaria* make color splashes visible for miles.

Tufts of bunch-grass and bear's-grass, the tall reed-like growth which furnishes the coil of Papago basketry, may be found contesting the steep bajadas with globose, downy-white brittle-brush, which in the fore-summer makes a golden glow of bloom. About this season, too, the crêpe-petaled thistle poppy, the "fried-egg flower" of the cow-boy, makes a lovely whiteness over sandy patches, persisting on into the Inner Bone Month of the Papago winter. But none of these things are on a scale to modify the effect of monotony in the country of the social shrubs. It is not until the lowest, most arid levels are reached that the yellowish greens of the creosote, mesquite, and palo-verde are relieved by the silvery-bluish grays of the ironwood, hackberry, *hohoba*, and *garamboya*. The ironwood you will know by its stiff upright branching and its roundish, easily ruffled leaves, as well as by the quality of its wood, for which a special ax is sold in that region, called the ironwood ax. The hackberry has a cleaner trunk and a brushier habit of branching, and the *garamboya* is that dense, rounded heap of brittle gray leaf and twig, frequently as large as a Papago house, from which at nightfall you may hear the twitter of the plumed quail seeking, in its impenetrable shelter, safety from their worst enemy, the coyote. Perched on the low branches near the central stem, like some strange secret fruit, they spend the nights, and raise in perfect secrecy their young broods.

The *hohoba* is a shrub conspicuous in its dull-green leafage, but important not to be missed by the traveler unacquainted with the resources of the arid regions, since it produces an extremely palatable nut, to the quality of which its native name, *hohoba*, youth-maker, is a sufficient tribute.

All this is to be observed between the beginning of winter rains and the hot fore-summer when from bristling leaf clusters the yuccas and agaves send up tall stalks that break, often in a space of hours, into long panicles of waxen white and yellow bells. Loveliest of all, the thousand-flowered maguey, wife of Sekala Ka'amja, whom the Hot Wind stole away.

It is not only the agaves and the yuccas that are wind-sown and wind-fertilized, but practically all the plants that give character to the arid region, the creosote, mesquite, acacia, palo-verde, the desert willow, the poplars lining the streamways, the walnuts at the bottoms of steep cañons, the batamote, whose surprising silver leafage, springing out of dead stems, betrays the presence of underground moisture, are raped of their virgin bloom by the seducing wind. Sometimes, when the rains have come quick and crowding under strong suns, streams of all but invisible pollen may be discovered on the moving air.

Later, the seed of wind-wrung bloom is blown about as down, or left rustling along the sand in dry pods and capsules, until in the Deathless Round of Life it comes to leaf and flower again. Long after the wind has passed, the tall flower-stalks of the yuccas and agaves remain upright, blanched white, and the Indians gather them to use for the pole-and-ring game, by the skilful playing of which, according to the later myth, Sekala Ka'amja won back the maiden flowers again. There is always a great dust raised by this seasonal chase of the Hot Wind, fine yellow dust of the *playas*, so that between the dust and the heat-quavers the whole landscape is veiled, and the mountains shadowed by the great fleeces of cumulus blown up from the California Gulf.

Thus the wind and the dust work together, for the fine silt of the wind rivers, when it falls, covers the seed the wind sows, and many of the winter-blooming varieties of flowering herbs, such as the cassia and verbena and the borages, will make a second growth and bloom, following the summer solstice. If the *temporales* are heavy enough, seeds of the social shrubs will germinate and often make sufficient growth to enable them to maintain themselves through the autumn drought till the turn of the sun in the south. It is the summer rains that sweeten the mesquite pods and fill out the corn. They also bring to quick maturity plants that require much heat with their drink, such as the wild pumpkin, whose silvery pubescent leaves gathered in close plats, tips pointed resolutely at the sun, may be seen increasing hourly in the exposed sandy bottoms. At this season the gourd runs and climbs by ropy stems, from which, late in November, after the leaves are off, lovely golden balls may be seen swinging from branches of the mesquite and acacia.

The summer rainy season is seldom prolonged beyond the middle of August. Then the land assumes again that aspect of life defeated which is the accepted note of desertness. This, since it is the season at which the roads, no longer exposed to the ravages of summer torrents, are likely to be safest, is the time at which the desert is usually traversed. For this reason the casual traveler is likely to come away from the country below the Rim without learning that, to the initiate, the secret charm of the desert is the secret of life triumphant [pp. 49–56].

Not all the country that the cactus takes, belongs to it. That gipsy of the tribe, the prickly-pear, goes as far east and north on the great plains as the Spanish adventurer ever went, perhaps farther. It goes as a rarity into Old World gardens, runs wild and thrives wherever there are sun and sand to bring its particular virtues into play. For the virtue of all cacti is that they represent the ultimate adaptations of vegetative life on its way up from its primordial home in the sea shallows, to the farthest, driest land. The prickly-pears — *Opuntia* is their family name, and the connection is a large one — run to arid wastes as gipsies do to the wilds, not because there the environment is the only one which will tolerate them, but because it is the one in which all the cactus tribe find themselves fulfilled, triumphant.

Here, in the country below the Mogollon Rim, the business of plants in making this a livable world, goes on all open to the light, not covered and confused by the multiplicity of its manifestations, as in the lush, well-rained-on lands. Here, in this veritable corner of southwestern Arizona, it has traveled the perfect round, from the filmed protoplasmic cell, by all the paths of plant

complexity, to the high simplicity of the great king cactus, the sahuaro.

Going west by the Old Trails Road, you do not begin to find sahuaro until you are well down toward the black hills of Tucson,
and it is not at its best this side of the toad-like heap of volcanic
trap which turns the river out of its course, called Tummomoc.
Here it rises to a height of twenty-five or thirty feet, erect, columnar, dull green, and deeply fluted, the outer ridges of the flutings set with rows of lateral spines that inclose it as in a delicate
grayish web. Between the ridges the sahuaro has a texture like
well-surfaced leather, giving back the light like spears, that,
seen from a rapidly moving car, make a continuous vertical
flicker in the landscape. Marching together against the rose-and-
vermilion evening, they have a stately look, like the pillars of
ruined temples.

For the first hundred years or so the sahuaro preserves the outline of its virgin intention to be straight, but in the case of wound-
ing, or perhaps in seasons of excess, it puts forth without calcu-
lation immense columnar branches like the arms of candelabra,
curving to bring their growing tips parallel to the axis of the main
stem, which they reproduce as if from their own roots.

The range of the sahuaro is restricted. Beginning with isolated
specimens about the San Pedro River, it spreads south and west,
but the true sahuaro forests are not reached until the gate of Papagueria is past, on the flats of Salt River. A small plantation of
them has crossed the Colorado and established itself in California. South they pass into Sonora as far as Altár, and approach al-

most to the gulf shore, where they are replaced by the still more majestic *sowesa*.

The leafless, compact outline of the sahuaro, its erect habit and indurated surfaces give it a secret look. Surmounting the crest of one of these denuded desert ranges, or marching up nearly vertical slopes without haste or stooping, or pushing its way imperturbably toward the sun from the midst of cat-claw and mesquite and palo-verde, it has the effect of being forever outside the community of desert life. Yet such is the succulence of its seedlings, that few of them would survive the first two or three seasons without the shelter of the spiny undergrowth. Once the recurved spines have spread and stiffened across the smooth, infolded intervals, the sahuaro is reasonably safe, even from the hard-mouthed cattle of the desert ranges. In very dry years, small rodents will gnaw into the flutings as far up as they can creep between the spines. High up out of reach of all marauders, the woodpecker drills his holes in the pulpy outer mass; but against these the sahuaro protects itself by surrounding its wounds with pockets of woody fiber woven to the shape of the woodpecker's burrow.

Indians of that country will often remove these pocket linings before the fiber has hardened, and make use of them for household containers, or you may find them kicking about the sand, hard as oak-knots, long after the sahuaro that wove them has sloughed off its outer layer in decay. For the woodpecker never penetrates to the sahuaro core, inclosed as it is in a tube of woody, semi-detached ribs which remain standing long after the spongy masses that fill and surround it have completely desiccated, slowly fraying out outward from the top as the ribs part, until at last the Papago carries them away to roof his house or his family tomb.

In the vast *abras* of southern Arizona, there is no woody growth capable of furnishing the woodpecker with the cool, dark house in which he brings up his broods. In a single unbranched sahuaro near Casa Grande, this year, I counted seventeen woodpeckers' holes, ranged up and down like the little openings of the cliff-dwellers' caves. Frequently the vacated apartments of the sahuaro skyscraper will be occupied by the pygmy owl, who may have made a meal of the eggs or young birds before he established his own family there. Everywhere, from the sahuaro towers, little blue-headed hawks may be seen perching, or, from the vantage of their height, launching swift predatory flights. But when in the crotch of some three-hundred-year-old specimen the fierce red-tail has made his nest, you will find all that neighborhood vacant of bird life.

It is not easy to take the life of a sahuaro, even when, just to see the tiny wavering flame run up the ridges, you set a match to the rows of oily spines. Even uprooted, as it may be in torrential seasonal rains, the prostrate column has unmeasured powers of living on its stored waters, and making an upward turn of its growing tip. One such I found at the back of Indian Oasis, toward Topohua, which had turned and budded after what must have been several seasons of overthrow.

If the column is by any accident broken, lateral branches start from the wound and curve upward toward the sun. Successive dry years constrict its columnar girth, as successive wet ones

Mary Austin

swell it, tracing in the undulations of the vertical outline, a record
of three or four centuries of rains. Around Tucson there must be
sahuaros that could tell what sort of weather it was the year Father Kino came to the founding of San Xavier, and at Salt River
I made my siesta under one that could have given a better guess
than any of our archæologists at what became of the ancient civ-
ilizations of Casa Grande and Los Muertos.

For I suppose the sahuaro harvest, and the ceremonial making
of sahuaro wine to be the oldest food festival of the cactus country. In the excavations of the buried cities of the Great-house culture, buried before the queen was born whose jewels opened the
portals of the West, they found little brown jars hermetically
sealed with clay, after the fashion in which Papago housewives
preserve sahuaro syrup at Cobabi and Quitovaquita.

From the month of the Cold Touching Mildly to the Inner
Bone Month of the winter, the flutings of sahuaro stems are
folded deep. With the first of the rains they begin to expand, until, if the season is propitious, the smooth leathery surfaces are
tight as drums. In May, on the blunt crowns, on the quarter most
exposed to the sun, buds appear like clusters of green figs, close-
packed as if in a platter. About this time red-tailed hawks, in their
shelterless nests in the tallest crotches, will be hatching their
young, and the quail in pairs going house-hunting in and out of
the *garamboyas*. Within a week or two the green fig-shaped buds
open, one by one, in filmy white-rayed circles, deep-yellow
hearted, the haunt of innumerable flies. By the latter part of June
or July the delicate corollas are replaced by fig-shaped fruits that

as they curl open when fully ripe, revealing the full-seeded, crimson pulp, have the effect of a second vivid flowering.

Just before the fruits burst, however, the Pima and Papago women turn out by villages to harvest them with long hooks made of a sahuaro rib and a crosspiece of acacia twig. Often, to save labor, they will peel the fruit as they collect it; returning at night with their great jars and baskets overflowing with the luscious juicy pulp. For this, and for all that I have written of the sahuaro festival in Papagueria, it is counted a crime to destroy a sahuaro.

There is a singular charm of the sahuaro forest, a charm of elegance, as the wind, moving like royalty across the well-spaced intervals, receives the courtesies of ironwood and ocotilla and palo-verde. It begins with the upright next-of-blood, with a stately rocking of the tall pillars on their roots, and a soft *ss-ss-ss* of the wind along their spiny ridges. Suddenly the bright blossom-tips of the ocotilla take flight like flocks of scarlet birds, as the long wands bow and recover in the movement of the wind, and after an appreciable interval the thin-leaved ironwood rustles and wrestles with it, loth to let it go, until it drops with almost a sullen note to the stiff whisper of the palo-verde, while the creosote fairly casts its forehead to the ground.

The ocotilla is not a true cactus, but belongs rather by nature of its adaptations to the fellowship of the mesquite and that leafless thorny shrub often found in its neighborhood, called *corona de Jesús*. It does not store moisture as the cactus does, but remains in the long seasons between the rains in a state of complete aridivation, putting forth miraculously after the first showers, at the ends of its branches, crowded panicles of bloom like the bloody tips of spears. The gray, thorny wands of the ocotilla, growing from ten to fifteen feet, brought together in a lovely vase form by the central stem, a few inches from the ground, are leafless for all but a brief season, when perhaps the first sign of spring is the flush of green creeping up their swaying lengths, in the shape of thin, blunt emerald leaves. After the leaves fall away, the petiole which supports them becomes a spine, for the sake of which the stems of ocotilla are used for chicken-fences and corrals, thickset in the ground, from which, as the spring comes around, they take heart of life, growing delicately green and scarlet-tipped again.

Ocotilla and sahuaro are to be found growing together on the gravelly slopes of the *abras*, and with them the bisnaga or barrel-cactus, which the stranger frequently mistakes for a young sahuaro. It has the same fluted, branchless, columnar habit, but the bisnaga is a darker green, its spines frequently reddish, its circumference larger, and its height seldom equal to the height of a man. It may also be distinguished from other cacti by having the axis of its growth, like the pointer of a dial, angling directly toward the sun. It is only when the observer finds several bisnagas growing together that the uniform slant begins to appear something more than an accident.

Now it is discovered that there is a crumpling of the surfaces toward the downthrow, and a half-turn of the flutings around the axis of growth, as if the plants had all been pulled by an irresistible force, out of their intention to grow symmetrically plump and upright. It seems probable that this disturbance of the barrel-shaped bulk is due to the more rapid evaporation of the side next to the sun; for the bisnaga is nothing, really, but a huge capsule of vegetable pulp, distended by the water which it collects and carries with the utmost parsimony from rain to rain. When the rains cease, it has been known to subsist on its own stores for a dozen years. Anywhere along the flood basins you are likely to see plump specimens of bisnaga uprooted from the rain-softened soil by their own weight, going on comfortably with their life processes while lying on one side. . . .

But after the great sahuaro, it is only the opuntias that successfully modify the desert scene. Of these there are two general types, the flat-branched prickly-pears, and the round-jointed chollas. If I called the prickly-pear the gipsy of its tribe, it was not without recollecting that the gipsies have their queen in *Opuntia santa rita*, with its coin-shaped disks of grape red and electric blue, touched in the spring with a delicate silver sheen. *Santa rita* is, however, too shy a grower to compete, as a feature of the landscape, with the chollas, which have a tree-like form and a social habit.

Among the chollas, the unaccustomed eye will distinguish the "old-man," having a silvery-haired appearance from the sheaths of its dense covering of spines, from the deer-horn type, slender-jointed, sparsely spined, and with a tendency of the stems to take the general tone of its red or yellowish bloom. Both the old-man and the horned cholla have the habit of propagation by dropped joints, and the same facilities for distribution by hooking their easily detachable sections to passing animals. But it is only the silver-haired varieties, *Opuntia fulgida* and *Opuntia Bigelovii*, sowing themselves across the mesas in thick droves like sheep, that give character to the country below the Rim.

Chollas will grow, in favored localities, as high as a horse, but a peculiar sheep-like outline is achieved by the habit of the fruiting stems. The fruits, bright lemon yellow after inconspicuous bloom, are produced on the topmost boughs, but after setting, remain in place several years, during which a slow movement of the shaggy whitish branches takes place, to bring the fruiting joints closest to the ground on which they are finally cast. A plantation of cholla, which will sometimes cover acres, any plant of which might have sprung from the dropped joints of a single individual, is called a chollitál, place of the cholla, one of those expressive native terms which I mean to spell hereafter as it is pronounced, choyitál.

Between Tucson and Phœnix, south of the paved road, there is a vast cactus garden that I can never pass without crossing my fingers against its spell. Often in the midst of other employments I am seized with such a fierce backward motion of my mind toward it as must have beset Thoreau for his Walden when he had left it for the town. So that if I should disappear some day unaccountably from my accustomed places, leaving no trace, you might find me there in some such state as you read of in monkish tales, when one walked in the woods for an hour and found that centuries had passed. Look for me beyond the last spur of Santa Catalina, where there is a one-armed sahuaro having a hawk's nest in the crotch. Beyond that there is a plantation of thistle poppies on the tops of whose dusty green stems have perched whole flocks of white, wind-ruffled doves, always about to take flight and yet never freed. Then small droves of *Opuntia Bigelovii*, like lambs feeding with their tails between their legs; here and there a bis-naga, dial pointed above its moving shadow; silvery flocks of cholla, now and then a sahuaro pushing aside the acacia under which its youth survived, or a stiff, purple-flowered ironwood, and droves and droves of cholla leading down to the dry arroyo, from which at intervals arise green cages full of golden palo-verde flowers.

Inside the choyital, where ancient black trap overlaps the sand, there will be islands of needlegrass, preferred by the reddish-stemmed *Opuntia* which is called, from the manner of its branching, "staghorn," and dense, globose clumps of *Opuntia ar-buscula*. But far down the sandy middle strip, stooping low, you can see the sand thick sown with detached joints, awaiting, with a breathless effect of suspense, the rain that brings the chance to root and grow.

There is an extraordinary feeling of intimacy about the choyi-tal, where practically all the life goes on below the level of the ob-server's eye. The opuntias are seldom man-high, and the scant grass lends no cover to the intense activity of insect and small ro-dent life. Only the infrequent sahuaro lifts a bird-flight out of reach, and the wide-searching light pours unstinted around its meager shade.

In this country the chollas are the favorite nesting-places of birds. Early in April, before the sun renders the thin screen of spines inadequate, the thrush and the mocking-bird and the mourning-dove rear their broods on shallow platforms of twigs in the antlered tops of *Opuntia tetracantha*, and the cactus-wren weaves her thick balls of needle-grass in the spiniest depths of the "old-man" cholla. But this excess of safety has its dire results, for at the entrance of the long tunnel leading to the nest, the pygmy owl sits watching like a cat, and now and then one comes upon pitiful fragments of nestlings impaled on the cactus spines in their first clumsy, tumbling flight.

It is the cast joints of cholla which the kangaroo-rat drags about its runways, in mazes in which a coyote would hesitate to set its paw. The road-runner is also credited with using them to fence in a snake it has marked for its prey. Understand that I am familiar enough with the road-runner to believe anything I am told about it, but my observation would lead me to conclude that this fencing in of the prey would take place only after the snake's back is broken with a driving stroke of the long bill, and would have as its object the protection of the quarry from other marauders. Once I saw this sleek cock of the choyital kill a small striped snake by alternately skimming about it in circles until the victim coiled, and then striking at the moveless rings, once, and away again, until, with the snake's back broken in two places, a blow on the head stilled the wriggling length. Usually, however, you will see this *corredor del camino* catching lizards or picking up black pinacate-beetles such as you find in great numbers at certain seasons, standing on their heads in the sand.

Around the outskirts of the cactus gardens, the conical hills of the farmer-ants arise out of circular cleared spaces not more than a yard or two in diameter, though farther north I have seen them as much as twenty or thirty feet. After the first rains, around these clearings, spring up downy carpets of inch-high "Indian wheat," like hoar-frost, whose full-seeded heads are harvested by the ants the moment they are matured. Ripening underground, the husks expand, each one in its tiny ball of fluff, which is carried up and deposited by the farmers in a white, webby ring around the hill, where it lies until the wind carries it away. Warm days toward the end of April, when the heads are bursting fast in the hidden storehouses, you can see the white ring widen visibly, while the particles of fluff seem to boil out of the ant-heap of their own force.

Days like this there is a sense of the concentration of life in the choyital that is only partly accounted for by the movement of bird and insect life, intensified as it is by the withdrawal of the circling ranges behind successive veils of light and heat. By mid-morning the small furred folk are asleep in their stopped earths, the singing-birds retreat to their nests, the hawks rest in the shadows of the sahuaros, wings adroop, but the choyital does not sleep. Life gathers full at the brim of the cup, where any drop might overfill it, and there stays. When the drop falls, the arrested cycle of life triumphant begins again [pp. 119–33].

To appreciate a creosote plantation, one must be able to think of the individual shrub as having its tail waving about in the sun and wind, and its intelligence underground. Then the wide spacing of the growing crowns is explained by the necessary horizontal spread of the root system in search of the thin envelope of moisture around the loose particles of the gravelly soil. In the rainy season the roots drink by means of minute hairs that are cast off when the last drop has been absorbed, after which the soul of the creosote sits and waits.

Plants of this type will run successfully through the average rainfall from century to century, but for growths of a shorter life-cycle and a more exigent bloom, it has been important, possibly more important in the early Pleistocene than now, to meet conditions of great irregularity in the water-supply with water-storage. For this the yuccas and agaves developed in their pithy stems and the thickened bases of their bayonet-pointed leaves, storage-capacity that enables them to send up, with magical rapidity, great spikes of waxen bloom to grace the rainless years. The obvious difference between yucca and agave is that the yucca produces its blossom crown from a lateral bud, and may go on doing so for indefinite periods, but the agave blooms from the central stem, and, blooming, dies. The great *Agave Americana*, called the century-plant, is a visitor across our southern border, and out of its stored energies, —which by no means run the hundred years with which it is popularly credited, — it throws up, in the course of days, a flowering stalk three or four times the height of a man, bearing seven thousand flowers, in whose fragrance the whole life of the agave is exhaled.

It is the yellow-flowered *Agave Palmeri*, taken just before the expanding growth begins, while the leaf bases are still packed with the sugary substance of the flowering bud, that is the mescal of the Southwestern tribes. Anywhere about the three-thousand-

or four-thousand-foot levels of the mountains of southern Arizona you may come upon the pits where the mescal is roasted, or even surprise a group of Indians feasting on the nutritious but not very attractive mass. When I calculate the seasons through which, drop by drop, the agave has collected the material for its stately bloom, eating mescal is to me a good deal like eating a baby.

The long central stem of the yuccas enables them to make much more of a figure in the landscape, particularly the one known as "Joshua-tree," whose weird stalking forms can be found farthest afield in pure desertness, or the sotol (*Dasylirion Wheeleri*), whose dense plumes of long rapier-like, saw-edged leaves and tall pyramids of delicate racemes, are visible like companies of bandoliers far across the mesas. This sort holds its dried flower stalk aloft long after the fruit has been eaten and scattered by the birds; even on into the next season's bloom. There is a humbler variety which goes everywhere, like the prickly-pear, and, under the name of amole, furnishes those who know enough not to despise its narrow, yellowish, pointed leaf varieties, with an excellent fiber, and, from its roots, a substitute for soap. But the final, most successful experiment of the Vegetative Spirit on its way up from the sea-borders to the driest of dry lands, is the great sahuaro, *Carnegea gigantea*.

In the economy of the sahuaro, branch and twig have been reduced to spines, the green of its leaves absorbed into its skin. The need of woody fiber has been perfectly met by the stiff but stringy hollow cylinder of semi-detached ribs that hold the stem erect, and its storage-capacity rendered elastic by the fluted surfaces, swelling and contracting to the rhythm of evaporation and the intake of the thirsty roots. After successive wet seasons, new flutings are let into the surfaces, like gores in a skirt; or, after shortage, taken up with the neatness of long experience. By such mechanisms the cactus-plant surpasses the stone-crops, the "hen-and-chickens," the "live-forevers" of other arid regions, so that until some plant is found able to make water out of its gaseous constituents in the air, we may conclude that here in the great sahuaro, the Vegetative Spirit comes to rest. Here it has met and surmounted all the conditions that for our cycle, menace, on this planet, the vegetative type. Passing, I salute it in the name of the exhaustless Powers of Life [pp. 137–40].

The first I knew of it was as a dim blue streak, shadow of a shadow, far east from the cinder-colored ranges of Lost Borders, its contours winding like a river, fixed in a motionless unreality. Above it fled a river of shimmering cloud between viewless shores of air, toward which our Paiute swamper, Tinnemaha, would look inquiringly whenever I asked him for a forecast of the weather. Not until, by that mysterious certainty Indians have of what is going on in you, he understood that I had recognized it as the Grand Cañon, did he tell me what the Paiutes believed of how it came to be just there, on the eastern rim of the country where their own borders ran out in unmapped desertness [p. 397].

The Land of Journeys' Ending

Half-way down to the turn which sets the great dragon cañon sprawling across the corner of Arizona, the eastern wall gives way for the *entrada* of the Little Colorado. It arrives from western New Mexico, from the Sierra Zuñi, having drawn in that silver thread along whose course arises the Middle Antheap of the World, fed also by small rivulets going north from the rim of the Mogollon Mesa, and the infrequent floods of Moencopie Wash. From Winslow, north, it cuts behind the San Francisco Mountains and skirts the Painted Desert on the west.

This Coloradito is a true desert river, flowing wide and shallowly, eating new courses in the treeless valleys with every heavy rain, or scuttling under its own sands in drought like a frightened *azotl*. Not until it reaches the sandstone formation of the Coconino plateau does it bite down to the level of the Colorado Grande.

The number of persons who can speak with personal knowledge of the river between the *entrada* of the Little Colorado and the lower end of Boulder Cañon may be counted on the fingers of one hand: Dellenbaugh, Stanton, the Kolb brothers; perhaps some others, men whose business is with areonoid and rod. From point to point of the plateau one sees how the river runs, sometimes between a sheer wall and a shallow bank of sand, with strips and splashes of greenness, but oftener at the bottom of a trough of detritus from which the striated cliffs rise sheer to the sky-line. In

Mary Austin

Marble Cañon it goes without shores, between straight-sided, gleaming walls; vermilion and ocher, blue and saffron, like the sections of petrified wood one smuggles out of Adamana.

On still days the air is shaken with the roaring sound of the water forced through the narrows, audible far back from the brink of the cañon. Where the walls recede, the river shows opaque and yellowish, like a celluloid river in a panorama, with faint flecks of light and motion, difficult to translate into the proper terms of raging rapids. Now and again it disappears in the black gash of the inner cañon toward Sipapu.

That very point at the crossing of Bright Angel Trail is the Hole in the Ground out of which, in the Days of the New, the Hopi came. From Hermit Rim the river writhes like a snake that, raging desperately against the steady up-push of the land, has stuck its fangs into its own side. For this river that drains an area about equal to the Republic of France does not proceed after the manner of rivers, seeking the land's lowest place. Not, at least, after it strikes the Colorado plateau.

This is a vast orderly country once laid down on the denuded earth-core as sea-bottom, now lying through almost its whole extent, more than a mile above sea-level. By many steep bajadas or meandering lines of castellated cliffs, tracing the flexures and fractures of its structural swells, it is divided into subsidiary plateaus, having each its own special interest. It was laid down in thousand-foot bands of limestone and shale, red, ocherous, sea-gray, and green, and so remains, tilted slightly toward the axis of the up-thrust. West, it runs to the palisades of the Virgin River beyond which the California desert drops two to three thousand

The Land of Journeys' Ending

feet. East of the Grand Cañon the plateau tilts down to the foot of Echo Cliffs, breaking high and abruptly between Marble Cañon and Moencopie Wash. Across this series of tilted tablelands, all the while that it was being slowly pushed skyward, the Rio Colorado cut its way.

Against the steady gnawing of the river, rose the land, as a log is pushed against a moving saw. Below the *entrada* of the Little Colorado, there must have been times when the land rose faster than the river could eat through the marble walls. Here the evidence of its balked fury stuns appreciation. Beyond this point, the river bends about the south front of Kaibab plateau, rising almost half a mile above the Marble Cañon country, which dips eastward here, and loses itself under the painted mesas. West of Kaibab lies Kanab; farthest west Shivwits, where the Shivwits Paiutes still cling to their ancestral home. Between them lie Shimuno [*sic*] and Uinkaret. These face you darkly from the Coconino plateau which rims the cañon on the south.

It is from Coconino that the cañon is best taken as a spectacle. But not from any one point do you immediately come into relation with it. Go back among the dark cedars and the widely spaced yellow pines until your feet find by instinct the slightly sloping ground that drops off suddenly into the abyss. Here you find yourself at the head of one of the triangular bays following the surface drainage inland to the farthest point at which it can gather erosive force. So now you perceive the structure of the Grand Cañon to be that of a true valley, kept narrow and straight-sided by the stubborn nature of its walls. Over toward Bright Angel, where the material is softer, it makes a gentler slope, or gets

Mary Austin

down from Kanab and Shimiuno [*sic*] by broken stairs and vast amphitheaters facing the lowest land.

The thing to marvel at about the Grand Cañon, is that man should find it so in his nature to be astounded by the thousand-foot reach of a valley wall only when it happens to be arranged vertically in space. The towhee, the junco, and the piñonero flit ceaselessly over the rim and back again. The whisk-tailed squirrels are no more fearful of falling into that awful gulf than you are of dropping into interplanetary space. You wonder why we so constantly adjure children to be "too big to be afraid," when it is evidently a much happier state to be too small to be. The cedar and the white-fringed mountain mahogany go over, seeking down sheer walls and along the many-hued talus their familiar levels. On the Tonto plateau they give place to sage-brush, and next to the feather-foliaged greasewood. Far down on the hot zone of the lowest cañon levels, the yuccas and agaves consort with the dust-colored cat-claw and the cacti. On the north rim, where living streams come down the rocky stairs, they bring with them all the bloom and the bird song whose succession makes the charm of long mountain slopes. Caught all at once in this vertical sweep, it fixes forever the standard of comparison for men whose constant measure is of up-and-downness.

There must be something in this way of seeing things that is native to the deepest self of man, for once it is seen, there is no way afterward of not seeing it. Any time now, — and sometimes whether I will or no, — by a mere turn of attention, over the shoulder of my mind, as it were, I see it there . . . as I loved most to see it, . . . the noiseless dance of island towers, advancing, retreat-

ing; . . . cliffs burning red from within; the magical, shifty shadows, the vast down-throw of Kaibab, grape-colored, with a
bloom on it of refracted light, . . . the twin, ember-glowing
towers between which in the last day all the Navajos will come
riding, riding down to Sipapu; old chiefs and older, he who broke
the Chaco towns, lance-armed raiders, shield on elbow from the
Shiprock region, fierce renegades from El Bosque Redondo,
brass-buttoned cavalry scouts, wound-striped khaki from
Château-Thierry, . . . riding, riding, red fire in the west and
shadows blue as morning [pp. 415–21].

Is the impulse which most people confess to, on first seeing the
Grand Cañon, to cast themselves into its dim violet depths,
confidently as a bird launches itself from a mountain-top upon
the air, a reawakened pulse of surety we once had of its being as
good a thing and as joyous to go down with the Left Hand as to
go up with the Right? It is at any rate, here, a magnificent thing.

The sage-brush-covered platform which you see from El To-
var, called Tonto plateau, is actually the surface of that scoured
granite core on which the whole of Kaibab foundation was laid.
It is a matter of three hours or less to go down to it, and so on
down into the V-shaped, inner cañon which the river has cut in
the most ancient rock.

There you see the frothy yellow flood making hidden bars of
sand and spewing them forth in boiling fountains of fury, like a
man ridding himself of nursed, secret grudges in spouts of tem-

per. But you will do better in the way of understanding what the Left Hand is about, if you stay on the rim and study the river of clouds to which you are made privy on Kaibab and Coconino. They come up burdened and shepherdless from the delta until they strike the lift of desert-heated air above Yuma and the Salada plains. They lift great glittering sails from the Pacific, defiling between the pillars of San Jacinto and San Bernardino.

Up and up they climb the viewless stairs, growing diaphanous until at last they have hid themselves in the deeps of the middle heavens. About the intervening peaks you see them glimmer into visibility and disappear, as though mountains had the power some people claim to exercise over the passing dead, of compelling them to materialize.

Going north to find the Colorado Front, that will release them into rain again, they are caught in the eddies that play about the Grand Cañon. Here acres of naked rock give back the sun with such intensity it burns the hand to touch, and the middle depth of the gorge is blue with the quiver of heat-waves, rising. Then the cold air from Kaibab comes sliding down the russet-hued slope, and in the currents thus set in motion, whole flocks of dove-breasted clouds are netted. Sometimes they are packed close from rim to rim and in the whirl of hot and cold, struggle woundedly between the walls. Then the lightning bounds back and back from sheer rock surfaces, and the thunder loses itself in its own echo.

After such intervals, sometimes, the upper levels will be fleecy soft with snow, through which, far down, you can see the dust-colored cat-claw and the hot banks on which the gila monster sprawls; for never, never do the clouds get down to the river except they have been to the mountain and resolved themselves in rain. On that business almost any day you will see them feeling their way cautiously among the rock towers, or catch them of early mornings resting just under the Rim, behind some tall potrero.

I recall catching a flock of them there one morning, wing-folded under Yavapi Point, as I came in from watching a gibbous moon walking the Rim cautiously like a pregnant woman. I had walked too far, watching the moonlight drip down salient ledges, and the tops of the potreros swim into view out of abysmal darkness like young worlds appearing, so that moonset found me where I thought it safest to wait until the dawn came up, as it does in the Navajo country, a turquoise horse, neighing joyously.

So as I passed Yavapi, I saw the cloud flock sleeping, as I have seen seal sleep with their noses resting on a point of rock, swaying with the sea's motion. More lightly still the clouds slept, until, as if my step had startled them, they began to scatter and rise, feeling for the wind's way, taking hands when they had found it, curling up and over the rim. Almost immediately I heard, far below, the soft *hee-haw* of the little wild burros, long-eared like rabbits, rabbit-colored, coming to drink of the dew, in the pits of the rocks where the clouds had rested. It was almost at this same place that I saw on another occasion the dim face of Rainbow Boy, behind the cloud-film in the rainbow halo. I am not sure that the other tourists saw anything but the changing configuration of the cliff through the cloud-drift, but that was their misfortune. It is only as they please that Those Above show themselves in the rainbow, which when the sun is low is perfectly round here, or the moonbow, faint and fluctuating on the level floor of cloud below the cañon rim [pp. 422–25].

Since the custodian put up the fence around it, nothing has come to Inscription Rock but an intermittent tourist stream, requiring federal enactment to prevent it from destroying one of the most interesting of southwestern landmarks, with that strange passion of the touring American, not so much to see notable places as to prove to other people that he has seen them. It is curious to note how much more character there is in the ancient Spanish inscriptions than in such modern print-cut names as have been allowed to remain. Even so, I suspect, the quality that the conquistadores wrote into the land, as they passed by here, will outlast the brisk conventionalized pattern stamped over it since 1848. If I did not believe this, I should not so wish that I could make my home here, in one of the ancient plazas on the Rock. Now, however, having accustomed myself to walk a mile and a half, mostly straight up in the air, for my daily drink, and carrying my marketing home on my head, I suppose that would not be convenient, though I can think of no place more suited to my purpose. But if not to live, then, perhaps, equally to my purpose to be buried here; and from my dust would spring the crêpe-petaled argemone.

Here, at least, I shall haunt, and as the time-streams bend and swirl about the Rock, I shall see again all the times that I have

The Land of Journeys' Ending

loved, and know certainly all that now I guess at. I shall hear the drums far down in the dancing-place, and talk with feather-venders going up to Chaco and the cliff dwellings of Cañon de Chelly. I shall see the Fire Dance on the top of Toyoállanne, and know what was in the hearts of the men of Pecos when they came down to Hawikuh in 1540. You, of a hundred years from now, if when you visit the Rock, you see the cupped silken wings of the argemone burst and float apart when there is no wind; or if, when all around is still, a sudden stir in the short-leaved pines, or fresh eagle feathers blown upon the shrine, that will be I, making known in such fashion as I may the land's undying quality [pp. 230–31].

John Muir

The Grand Cañon
of the Colorado

*J*ohn Muir wrote many magazine articles and short pieces, and many of these centered on specific areas as does this 1902 essay about the Grand Canyon. On one of Muir's trips to the Grand Canyon he journeyed with John Burroughs. Both Muir and Burroughs were in their early sixties, and the two naturalists looked much alike—tall, with long white patriarchal beards—but there the resemblance ended. Burroughs personified the eastern and Muir the western approach to landscape. Burroughs was exhausted by Muir's energy and then had to endure being chastised for not keeping up. He became so exasperated with Muir's continual chatter that he opined it would be nice if Muir were dropped into the abyss so he, Burroughs, could have a little peace and quiet.

Interestingly enough in this account of a Grand Canyon trip, there are surprising and careless botanical errors from a writer whose first love was botany. Cereus giganteus, *the saguaro cactus, does not grow in the Grand Canyon, nor do the "tree yuccas," the Joshua trees endemic to the Mojave Desert. Nor are there prehistoric irrigation ditches in the canyon. Otherwise it is an orderly piece, beginning with an overview and then getting down to specifics and individual views, to separate times of day. Muir traveled down to the river and his description of the altitudinal change in plants and animals is enlivened by accounts of the quixotic weather effects remarked by anyone who has spent any time in the canyon. As is his wont, the descriptive passages are full of vitality and spirit: Muir never met a landscape he couldn't rhapsodize about.*

John Muir

Happy nowadays is the tourist, with earth's wonders, new and old, spread invitingly open before him, and a host of able workers as his slaves making everything easy, padding plush about him, grading roads for him, boring tunnels, moving hills out of his way, eager, like the devil, to show him all the kingdoms of the world and their glory and foolishness, spiritualizing travel for him with lightning and steam, abolishing space and time and almost everything else. Little children and tender, pulpy people, as well as storm-seasoned explorers, may now go almost everywhere in smooth comfort, cross oceans and deserts scarce accessible to fishes and birds, and, dragged by steel horses, go up high mountains, riding gloriously beneath starry showers of sparks, ascending like Elijah in a whirlwind and chariot of fire.

First of the wonders of the great West to be brought within reach of the tourist were the Yosemite and the Big Trees, on the completion of the first transcontinental railway; next came the Yellowstone and icy Alaska, by the Northern roads; and last the Grand Cañon of the Colorado, which, naturally the hardest to reach, has now become, by a branch of the Santa Fé, the most accessible of all.

Of course with this wonderful extension of steel ways through our wilderness there is loss as well as gain. Nearly all railroads are bordered by belts of desolation. The finest wilderness perishes as if stricken with pestilence. Bird and beast people, if not the dryads, are frightened from the groves. Too often the groves

The Grand Cañon of the Colorado

also vanish, leaving nothing but ashes. Fortunately, nature has a few big places beyond man's power to spoil — the ocean, the two icy ends of the globe, and the Grand Cañon.

When I first heard of the Santa Fé trains running to the edge of the Grand Cañon of Arizona, I was troubled with thoughts of the disenchantment likely to follow. But last winter, when I saw those trains crawling along through the pines of the Cocanini Forest and close up to the brink of the chasm at Bright Angel, I was glad to discover that in the presence of such stupendous scenery they are nothing. The locomotives and trains are mere beetles and caterpillars, and the noise they make is as little disturbing as the hooting of an owl in the lonely woods.

In a dry, hot, monotonous forested plateau, seemingly boundless, you come suddenly and without warning upon the abrupt edge of a gigantic sunken landscape of the wildest, most multitudinous features, and those features, sharp and angular, are made out of flat beds of limestone and sandstone forming a spiry, jagged, gloriously colored mountain-range countersunk in a level gray plain. It is a hard job to sketch it even in scrawniest outline; and try as I may, not in the least sparing myself, I cannot tell the hundredth part of the wonders of its features — the side-cañons, gorges, alcoves, cloisters, and amphitheaters of vast sweep and depth, carved in its magnificent walls; the throng of great architectural rocks it contains resembling castles, cathedrals, temples, and palaces, towered and spired and painted, some of them nearly a mile high, yet beneath one's feet. All this, however, is less difficult than to give any idea of the impression of wild, primeval beauty and power one receives in merely gazing from its brink.

John Muir

The view down the gulf of color and over the rim of its wonderful wall, more than any other view I know, leads us to think of our earth as a star with stars swimming in light, every radiant spire pointing the way to the heavens.

But it is impossible to conceive what the cañon is, or what impression it makes, from descriptions or pictures, however good. Naturally it is untellable even to those who have seen something perhaps a little like it on a small scale in this same plateau region. One's most extravagant expectations are indefinitely surpassed, though one expect much from what is said of it as "the biggest chasm on earth"—"so big is it that all other big things, — Yosemite, the Yellowstone, the Pyramids, Chicago, — all would be lost if tumbled into it." Naturally enough, illustrations as to size are sought for among other cañons like or unlike it, with the common result of worse confounding confusion. The prudent keep silence. It was once said that the "Grand Cañon could put a dozen Yosemites in its vest pocket."

The justly famous Grand Cañon of the Yellowstone is, like the Colorado, gorgeously colored and abruptly countersunk in a plateau, and both are mainly the work of water. But the Colorado's cañon is more than a thousand times larger, and as a score or two new buildings of ordinary size would not appreciably change the general view of a great city, so hundreds of Yellowstones might be eroded in the sides of the Colorado Cañon without noticeably augmenting its size or the richness of its sculpture. But it is not true that the great Yosemite rocks would be thus lost or hidden. Nothing of their kind in the world, so far as I know, rivals El Capitan and Tissiack, much less dwarfs or in any way belittles them.

The Grand Cañon of the Colorado

None of the sandstone or limestone precipices of the cañon that I have seen or heard of approaches in smooth, flawless strength and grandeur the granite face of El Capitan or the Tenaya side of Cloud's Rest. These colossal cliffs, types of permanence, are about three thousand and six thousand feet high; those of the cañon that are sheer are about half as high, and are types of fleeting change; while glorious-domed Tissiack, noblest of mountain buildings, far from being overshadowed or lost in this rosy, spiry cañon company, would draw every eye, and, in serene majesty, "aboon them a'" she would take her place — castle, temple, palace, or tower. Nevertheless a noted writer, comparing the Grand Cañon in a general way with the glacial Yosemite, says: "And the Yosemite — ah, the lovely Yosemite! Dumped down into the wilderness of gorges and mountains, it would take a guide who knew of its existence a long time to find it." This is striking, and shows up well above the levels of commonplace description; but it is confusing, and has the fatal fault of not being true. As well try to describe an eagle by putting a lark in it. "And the lark — ah, the lovely lark! Dumped down the red, royal gorge of the eagle, it would be hard to find." Each in its own place is better, singing at heaven's gate, and sailing the sky with the clouds.

Every feature of nature's big face is beautiful, — height and hollow, wrinkle, furrow, and line, — and this is the main master furrow of its kind on our continent, incomparably greater and more impressive than any other yet discovered, or likely to be discovered, now that all the great rivers have been traced to their heads.

The Colorado River rises in the heart of the continent on the dividing ranges and ridges between the two oceans, drains thousands of snowy mountains through narrow or spacious valleys, and thence through cañons of every color, sheer-walled and deep, all of which seem to be represented in this one grand cañon of cañons.

It is very hard to give anything like an adequate conception of its size, much more of its color, its vast wall-sculpture, the wealth of ornate architectural buildings that fill it, or, most of all, the tremendous impression it makes. According to Major Powell, it is about two hundred and seventeen miles long, from five to fifteen miles wide from rim to rim, and from about five thousand to six thousand feet deep. So tremendous a chasm would be one of the world's greatest wonders even if, like ordinary cañons cut in sedimentary rocks, it were empty and its walls were simple. But instead of being plain, the walls are so deeply and elaborately carved into all sorts of recesses — alcoves, cirques, amphitheaters, and side-cañons — that were you to trace the rim closely around on both sides your journey would be nearly a thousand miles long. Into all these recesses the level, continuous beds of rock in ledges and benches, with their various colors, run like broad ribbons, marvelously beautiful and effective even at a distance of ten or twelve miles. And the vast space these glorious walls inclose, instead of being empty, is crowded with gigantic architectural rock forms gorgeously colored and adorned with towers and spires like works of art.

Looking down from this level plateau, we are more impressed with a feeling of being on the top of everything than when looking from the summit of a mountain. From side to side of the vast

The Grand Cañon of the Colorado

gulf, temples, palaces, towers, and spires come soaring up in thick array half a mile or nearly a mile above their sunken, hidden bases, some to a level with our standpoint, but none higher. And in the inspiring morning light all are so fresh and rosy-looking that they seem new-born; as if, like the quick-growing crimson snow-plants of the California woods, they had just sprung up, hatched by the warm, brooding, motherly weather.

In trying to describe the great pines and sequoias of the Sierra, I have often thought that if one of those trees could be set by itself in some city park, its grandeur might there be impressively realized; while in its home forests, where all magnitudes are great, the weary, satiated traveler sees none of them truly. It is so with these majestic rock structures.

Though mere residual masses of the plateau, they are dowered with the grandeur and repose of mountains, together with the finely chiseled carving and modeling of man's temples and palaces, and often, to a considerable extent, with their symmetry. Some, closely observed, look like ruins; but even these stand plumb and true, and show architectural forms loaded with lines strictly regular and decorative, and all are arrayed in colors that storms and time seem only to brighten. They are not placed in regular rows in line with the river, but "a' through ither," as the Scotch say, in lavish, exuberant crowds, as if nature in wildest extravagance held her bravest structures as common as gravel-piles. Yonder stands a spiry cathedral nearly five thousand feet in height, nobly symmetrical, with sheer buttressed walls and arched doors and windows, as richly finished and decorated with sculptures as the great rock temples of India or Egypt. Beside it rises a huge castle with arched gateway, turrets, watch-towers, ramparts, etc., and to right and left palaces, obelisks, and pyramids fairly fill the gulf, all colossal and all lavishly painted and carved. Here and there a flat-topped structure may be seen, or one imperfectly domed; but the prevailing style is ornate Gothic, with many hints of Egyptian and Indian.

Throughout this vast extent of wild architecture — nature's own capital city — there seem to be no ordinary dwellings. All look like grand and important public structures, except perhaps some of the lower pyramids, broad-based and sharp-pointed, covered with down-flowing talus like loosely set tents with hollow, sagging sides. The roofs often have disintegrated rocks heaped and draggled over them, but in the main the masonry is firm and laid in regular courses, as if done by square and rule.

Nevertheless they are ever changing: their tops are now a dome, now a flat table or a spire, as harder or softer strata are reached in their slow degradation, while the sides, with all their fine moldings, are being steadily undermined and eaten away. But no essential change in style or color is thus effected. From century to century they stand the same. What seems confusion among the rough earthquake-shaken crags nearest one comes to order as soon as the main plan of the various structures appears. Every building, however complicated and laden with ornamental lines, is at one with itself and every one of its neighbors, for the same characteristic controlling belts of color and solid strata extend with wonderful constancy for very great distances, and pass through and give style to thousands of separate structures, however their smaller characters may vary.

The Grand Cañon of the Colorado

Of all the various kinds of ornamental work displayed, — carving, tracery on cliff-faces, moldings, arches, pinnacles, — none is more admirably effective or charms more than the webs of rain-channeled taluses. Marvelously extensive, without the slightest appearance of waste or excess, they cover roofs and dome-tops and the base of every cliff, belt each spire and pyramid and massy, towering temple, and in beautiful continuous lines go sweeping along the great walls in and out around all the intricate system of side-cañons, amphitheaters, cirques, and scallops into which they are sculptured. From one point hundreds of miles of this fairy embroidery may be traced. It is all so fine and orderly that it would seem that not only had the clouds and streams been kept harmoniously busy in the making of it, but that every raindrop sent like a bullet to a mark had been the subject of a separate thought, so sure is the outcome of beauty through the stormy centuries. Surely nowhere else are there illustrations so striking of the natural beauty of desolation and death, so many of nature's own mountain buildings wasting in glory of high desert air — going to dust. See how steadfast in beauty they all are in their going. Look again and again how the rough, dusty boulders and sand of disintegration from the upper ledges wreathe in beauty the next and next below with these wonderful taluses, and how the colors are finer the faster the waste. We oftentimes see nature giving beauty for ashes, — as in the flowers of a prairie after fire, — but here the very dust and ashes are beautiful.

Gazing across the mighty chasm, we at last discover that it is not its great depth nor length, nor yet these wonderful buildings, that most impresses us. It is its immense width, sharply defined by precipitous walls plunging suddenly down from a flat plain, declaring in terms instantly apprehended that the vast gulf is a gash in the once unbroken plateau, made by slow, orderly erosion and removal of huge beds of rocks. Other valleys of erosion are as great, — in all their dimensions some are greater, — but none of these produces an effect on the imagination at once so quick and profound, coming without study, given at a glance. Therefore by far the greatest and most influential feature of this view from Bright Angel or any other of the cañon views is the opposite wall. Of the one beneath our feet we see only fragmentary sections in cirques and amphitheaters and on the sides of the outjutting promontories between them, while the other, though far distant, is beheld in all its glory of color and noble proportions — the one supreme beauty and wonder to which the eye is ever turning. For while charming with its beauty it tells the story of the stupendous erosion of the cañon — the foundation of the unspeakable impression made on everybody. It seems a gigantic statement for even nature to make, all in one mighty stone word, apprehended at once like a burst of light, celestial color its natural vesture, coming in glory to mind and heart as to a home prepared for it from the very beginning. Wildness so godful, cosmic, primeval, bestows a new sense of earth's beauty and size. Not even from high mountains does the world seem so wide, so like a star in glory of light on its way through the heavens.

I have observed scenery-hunters of all sorts getting first views of yosemites, glaciers, While Mountain ranges, etc. Mixed with the enthusiasm which such scenery naturally excites, there is often weak gushing, and many splutter aloud like little waterfalls. Here, for a few moments at least, there is silence, and all are in dead earnest, as if awed and hushed by an earthquake — perhaps until the cook cries "Breakfast!" or the stable-boy "Horses are ready!" Then the poor unfortunates, slaves of regular habits, turn quickly away, gasping and muttering as if wondering where they had been and what had enchanted them.

Roads have been made from Bright Angel Hotel through the Cocanini Forest to the ends of outstanding promontories, commanding extensive views up and down the cañon. The nearest of them, three or four miles east and west, are McNeil's Point and Rowe's Point; the latter, besides commanding the eternally interesting cañon, gives wide-sweeping views southeast and west over the dark forest roof to the San Francisco and Mount Trumbull volcanoes — the bluest of mountains over the blackest of level woods.

Instead of thus riding in dust with the crowd, more will be gained by going quietly afoot along the rim at different times of day and night, free to observe the vegetation, the fossils in the rocks, the seams beneath overhanging ledges once inhabited by Indians, and to watch the stupendous scenery in the changing lights and shadows, clouds, showers, and storms. One need not go hunting the so-called "points of interest." The verge anywhere, everywhere, is a point of interest beyond one's wildest dreams.

As yet, few of the promontories or throng of mountain buildings in the cañon are named. Nor among such exuberance of forms are names thought of by the bewildered, hurried tourist. He would be as likely to think of names for waves in a storm. The

John Muir

Eastern and Western Cloisters, Hindu Amphitheater, Cape Royal, Powell's Plateau, and Grand View Point, Point Sublime, Bissell and Moran points, the Temple of Set, Vishnu's Temple, Shiva's Temple, Twin Temples, Tower of Babel, Hance's Column — these fairly good names given by Dutton, Holmes, Moran, and others are scattered over a large stretch of the cañon wilderness.

All the cañon rock-beds are lavishly painted, except a few neutral bars and the granite notch at the bottom occupied by the river, which makes but little sign. It is a vast wilderness of rocks in a sea of light, colored and glowing like oak and maple woods in autumn, when the sun-gold is richest. I have just said that it is impossible to learn what the cañon is like from descriptions and pictures. Powell's and Dutton's descriptions present magnificent views not only of the cañon but of all the grand region round about it; and Holmes's drawings, accompanying Dutton's report, are wonderfully good. Surely faithful and loving skill can go no further in putting the multitudinous decorated forms on paper. But the *colors*, the living, rejoicing *colors*, chanting morning and evening in chorus to heaven! Whose brush or pencil, however lovingly inspired, can give us these? And if paint is of no effect, what hope lies in pen-work? Only this: some may be incited by it to go and see for themselves.

No other range of mountainous rock-work of anything like the same extent have I seen that is so strangely, boldly, lavishly colored. The famous Yellowstone Cañon below the falls comes to mind, but, wonderful as it is, and well deserved as is its fame,

The Grand Cañon of the Colorado

compared with this it is only a bright rainbow ribbon at the roots of the pines. Each of the series of level, continuous beds of carboniferous rocks of the cañon has, as we have seen, its own characteristic color. The summit limestone-beds are pale yellow; next below these are the beautiful rose-colored cross-bedded sandstones; next there are a thousand feet of brilliant red sandstones; and below these the red wall limestones, over two thousand feet thick, rich massy red, the greatest and most influential of the series, and forming the main color-fountain. Between these are many neutral-tinted beds. The prevailing colors are wonderfully deep and clear, changing and blending with varying intensity from hour to hour, day to day, season to season; throbbing, wavering, glowing, responding to every passing cloud or storm, a world of color in itself, now burning in separate rainbow bars streaked and blotched with shade, now glowing in one smooth, all-pervading ethereal radiance like the alpenglow, uniting the rocky world with the heavens.

The dawn, as in all the pure, dry desert country, is ineffably beautiful; and when the first level sunbeams sting the domes and spires, with what a burst of power the big, wild days begin! The dead and the living, rocks and hearts alike, awake and sing the new-old song of creation. All the massy headlands and salient angles of the walls, and the multitudinous temples and palaces, seem to catch the light at once, and cast thick black shadows athwart hollow and gorge, bringing out details as well as the main massive features of the architecture; while all the rocks, as if wild with life, throb and quiver and glow in the glorious sunburst, rejoicing. Every rock temple then becomes a temple of music; every spire and pinnacle an angel of light and song, shouting color halleluiahs.

As the day draws to a close, shadows, wondrous, black, and thick, like those of the morning, fill up the wall hollows, while the glowing rocks, their rough angles burned off, seem soft and hot to the heart as they stand submerged in purple haze, which now fills the cañon like a sea. Still deeper, richer, more divine grow the great walls and temples, until in the supreme flaming glory of sunset the whole cañon is transfigured, as if all the life and light of centuries of sunshine stored up and condensed in the rocks was now being poured forth as from one glorious fountain, flooding both earth and sky.

Strange to say, in the full white effulgence of the midday hours the bright colors grow dim and terrestrial in common gray haze; and the rocks, after the manner of mountains, seem to crouch and drowse and shrink to less than half their real stature, and have nothing to say to one, as if not at home. But it is fine to see how quickly they come to life and grow radiant and communicative as soon as a band of white clouds come floating by. As if shouting for joy, they seem to spring up to meet them in hearty salutation, eager to touch them and beg their blessings. It is just in the midst of these dull midday hours that the cañon clouds are born.

A good storm-cloud full of lightning and rain on its way to its work on a sunny desert day is a glorious object. Across the cañon, opposite the hotel, is a little tributary of the Colorado called Bright Angel Creek. A fountain-cloud still better deserves the name "Angel of the Desert Wells" — clad in bright plumage, car-

The Grand Cañon of the Colorado

rying cool shade and living water to countless animals and plants ready to perish, noble in form and gesture, seeming able for anything, pouring life-giving, wonder-working floods from its alabaster fountains, as if some sky-lake had broken. To every gulch and gorge on its favorite ground is given a passionate torrent, roaring, replying to the rejoicing lightning—stones, tons in weight, hurrying away as if frightened, showing something of the way Grand Cañon work is done. Most of the fertile summer clouds of the cañon are of this sort, massive, swelling cumuli, growing rapidly, displaying delicious tones of purple and gray in the hollows of their sun-beaten bosses, showering favored areas of the heated landscape, and vanishing in an hour or two. Some, busy and thoughtful-looking, glide with beautiful motion along the middle of the cañon in flocks, turning aside here and there, lingering as if studying the needs of particular spots, exploring side-cañons, peering into hollows like birds seeking nest-places, or hovering aloft on outspread wings. They scan all the red wilderness, dispensing their blessings of cool shadows and rain where the need is the greatest, refreshing the rocks, their offspring as well as the vegetation, continuing their sculpture, deepening gorges and sharpening peaks. Sometimes, blending all together, they weave a ceiling from rim to rim, perhaps opening a window here and there for sunshine to stream through, suddenly lighting some palace or temple and making it flare in the rain as if on fire.

Sometimes, as one sits gazing from a high, jutting promontory, the sky all clear, showing not the slightest wisp or penciling, a bright band of cumuli will appear suddenly, coming up the cañon in single file, as if tracing a well-known trail, passing in review, each in turn darting its lances and dropping its shower, making a row of little vertical rivers in the air above the big brown one. Others seem to grow from mere points, and fly high above the cañon, yet following its course for a long time, noiseless, as if hunting, then suddenly darting lightning at unseen marks, and hurrying on. Or they loiter here and there as if idle, like laborers out of work, waiting to be hired.

Half a dozen or more showers may oftentimes be seen falling at once, while far the greater part of the sky is in sunshine, and not a raindrop comes nigh one. These thunder-showers from as many separate clouds, looking like wisps of long hair, may vary greatly in effects. The pale, faint streaks are showers that fail to reach the ground, being evaporated on the way down through the dry, thirsty air, like streams in deserts. Many, on the other hand, which in the distance seem insignificant, are really heavy rain, however local; these are the gray wisps well zigzagged with lightning. The darker ones are torrent rain, which on broad, steep slopes of favorable conformation give rise to so-called "cloud-bursts"; and wonderful is the commotion they cause. The gorges and gulches below them, usually dry, break out in loud uproar, with a sudden downrush of muddy, boulder-laden floods. Down they all go in one simultaneous gush, roaring like lions rudely awakened, each of the tawny brood actually kicking up a dust at the first onset.

During the winter months snow falls over all the high plateau, usually to a considerable depth, whitening the rim and the roofs of the cañon buildings. But last winter, when I arrived at Bright

The Grand Cañon of the Colorado

Angel in the middle of January, there was no snow in sight, and the ground was dry, greatly to my disappointment, for I had made the trip mainly to see the cañon in its winter garb. Soothingly I was informed that this was an exceptional season, and that the good snow might arrive at any time. After waiting a few days, I gladly hailed a broad-browed cloud coming grandly on from the west in big promising blackness, very unlike the white sailors of the summer skies. Under the lee of a rim-ledge, with another snow-lover, I watched its movements as it took possession of the cañon and all the adjacent region in sight. Trailing its gray fringes over the spiry tops of the great temples and towers, it gradually settled lower, embracing them all with ineffable kindness and gentleness of touch, and fondled the little cedars and pines as they quivered eagerly in the wind like young birds begging their mothers to feed them. The first flakes and crystals began to fly about noon, sweeping straight up the middle of the cañon, and swirling in magnificent eddies along the sides. Gradually the hearty swarms closed their ranks, and all the cañon was lost in gray gloom except a short section of the wall and a few trees beside us, which looked glad with snow in their needles and about their feet as they leaned out over the gulf. Suddenly the storm opened with magical effect to the north over the cañon of Bright Angel Creek, inclosing a sunlit mass of the cañon architecture, spanned by great white concentric arches of cloud like the bows of a silvery aurora. Above these and a little back of them was a series of upboiling purple clouds, and high above all, in the background, a range of noble cumuli towered aloft like snow-laden mountains, their pure pearl bosses flooded with sunshine. The whole noble picture, calmly glowing, was framed in thick gray gloom, which soon closed over it; and the storm went on, opening and closing until night covered all.

Two days later, when we were on a jutting point about eighteen miles east of Bright Angel and one thousand feet higher, we enjoyed another storm of equal glory as to cloud effects, though only a few inches of snow fell. Before the storm began we had a magnificent view of this grander upper part of the cañon and also of the Cocanini Forest and Painted Desert. The march of the clouds with their storm-banners flying over this sublime landscape was unspeakably glorious, and so also was the breaking up of the storm next morning — the mingling of silver-capped rock, sunshine, and cloud.

Most tourists make out to be in a hurry even here; therefore their few days or hours would be best spent on the promontories nearest the hotel. Yet a surprising number go down the Bright Angel trail to the brink of the inner gloomy granite gorge overlooking the river. Deep cañons attract like high mountains; the deeper they are, the more surely are we drawn into them. On foot, of course, there is no danger whatever, and, with ordinary precautions, but little on animals. In comfortable tourist faith, unthinking, unfearing, down go men, women, and children on whatever is offered, horse, mule, or burro, as if saying with Jean Paul, "fear nothing but fear" — not without reason, for these cañon trails down the stairways of the gods are less dangerous than they seem, less dangerous than home stairs. The guides are cautious, and so are the experienced, much-enduring beasts. The scrawniest Rosinantes and wizened-rat mules cling hard to the

The Grand Cañon of the Colorado

rocks endwise or sidewise, like lizards or ants. From terrace to terrace, climate to climate, down one creeps in sun and shade, through gorge and gully and grassy ravine, and, after a long scramble on foot, at last beneath the mighty cliffs one comes to the grand, roaring river.

To the mountaineer the depth of the cañon, from five thousand to six thousand feet, will not seem so very wonderful, for he has often explored others that are about as deep. But the most experienced will be awe-struck but the vast extent of strange, countersunk scenery, the multitude of huge rock monuments of painted masonry built up in regular courses towering above, beneath, and round about him. By the Bright Angel trail the last fifteen hundred feet of the descent to the river has to be made afoot down the gorge of Indian Garden Creek. Most of the visitors do not like this part, and are content to stop at the end of the horse-trail and look down on the dull-brown flood from the edge of the Indian Garden Plateau. By the new Hance trail, excepting a few daringly steep spots, you can ride all the way to the river, where there is a good spacious camp-ground in a mesquit-grove. This trail, built by brave Hance, begins on the highest part of the rim, eight thousand feet above the sea, a thousand feet higher than the head of Bright Angel trail, and the descent is a little over six thousand feet, through a wonderful variety of climate and life. Often late in the fall, when frosty winds are blowing and snow is flying at one end of the trail, tender plants are blooming in balmy summer weather at the other. The trip down and up can be made afoot easily in a day. In this way one is free to observe the scenery and vegetation, instead of merely clinging to his animal and watching its steps. But all who have time should go prepared to camp awhile on the riverbank, to rest and learn something about the plants and animals and the mighty flood roaring past. In cool, shady amphitheaters at the head of the trail there are groves of white silver fir and Douglas spruce, with ferns and saxifrages that recall snowy mountains; below these, yellow pine, nut-pine, juniper, hop-hornbeam, ash, maple, holly-leaved berberis, cowania, spiræa, dwarf oak, and other small shrubs and trees. In dry gulches and on taluses and sun-beaten crags are sparsely scattered yuccas, cactuses, agave, etc. Where springs gush from the rocks there are willow thickets, grassy flats, and bright flowery gardens, and in the hottest recesses the delicate abronia, mesquit, woody compositæ, and arborescent cactuses.

The most striking and characteristic part of this widely varied vegetation are the cactaceæ — strange, leafless, old-fashioned plants with beautiful flowers and fruit, in every way able and admirable. While grimly defending themselves with innumerable barbed spears, they offer both food and drink to man and beast. Their juicy globes and disks and fluted cylindrical columns are almost the only desert wells that never go dry, and they always seem to rejoice the more and grow plumper and juicier the hotter the sunshine and sand. Some are spherical, like rolled-up porcupines, crouching in rock hollows beneath a mist of gray lances, unmoved by the wildest winds. Others, standing as erect as bushes and trees or tall branchless pillars crowned with magnificent flowers, their prickly armor sparkling, look boldly abroad over the glaring desert, making the strangest forests ever seen or dreamed of. *Cereus giganteus*, the grim chief of the desert tribe, is

The Grand Cañon of the Colorado

often thirty or forty feet high in southern Arizona. Several species of tree yuccas in the same deserts, laden in early spring with superb while lilies, form forests hardly less wonderful, though here they grow singly or in small lonely groves. The low, almost stemless *Yucca baccata*, with beautiful lily-flowers and sweet banana-like fruit, prized by the Indians, is common along the cañon rim, growing on lean, rocky soil beneath mountain-mahogany, nut-pines, and junipers, beside dense flowery mats of *Spiræa cæspitosa* and the beautiful pinnate-leaved *Spiræa millefolium*. The nut-pine, *Pinus edulis*, scattered along the upper slopes and roofs of the cañon buildings, is the principal tree of the strange Dwarf Cocanini Forest. It is a picturesque stub of a pine about twenty-five feet high, usually with dead, lichened limbs thrust through its rounded head, and grows on crags and fissured rock tables, braving heat and frost, snow and drought, and continues patiently, faithfully fruitful for centuries. Indians and insects and almost every desert bird and beast come to it to be fed.

To civilized people from corn and cattle and wheat-field countries the cañon at first sight seems as uninhabitable as a glacier crevasse, utterly silent and barren. Nevertheless it is the home of a multitude of our fellow-mortals, men as well as animals and plants. Centuries ago it was inhabited by tribes of Indians, who, long before Columbus saw America, built thousands of stone houses in its crags, and large ones, some of them several stories high, with hundreds of rooms, on the mesas of the adjacent regions. Their cliff-dwellings, almost numberless, are still to be seen in the cañon, scattered along both sides from top to bottom and throughout its entire length, built of stone and mortar in seams and fissures like swallows' nests, or on isolated ridges and peaks. The ruins of larger buildings are found on open spots by the river, but most of them aloft on the brink of the wildest, giddiest precipices, sites evidently chosen for safety from enemies, and seemingly accessible only to the birds of the air. Many caves were also used as dwelling-places, as were mere seams on cliff-fronts formed by unequal weathering and with or without outer or side walls; and some of them were covered with colored pictures of animals. The most interesting of these cliff-dwellings had pathetic little ribbon-like strips of garden on narrow terraces, where irrigating-water could be carried to them — most romantic of sky-gardens, but eloquent of hard times.

In recesses along the river and on the first plateau flats above its gorge were fields and gardens of considerable size, where irrigating-ditches may still be traced. Some of these ancient gardens are still cultivated by Indians, descendants of cliff dwellers, who raise corn, squashes, melons, potatoes, etc., to reinforce the produce of the many wild food-furnishing plants, nuts, beans, berries, yucca and cactus fruits, grass and sunflower seeds, etc., and the flesh of animals, deer, rabbits, lizards, etc. The cañon Indians I have met here seem to be living much as did their ancestors, though not now driven into rock dens. They are able, erect men, with commanding eyes, which nothing that they wish to see can escape. They are never in a hurry, have a strikingly measured, deliberate, bearish manner of moving the limbs and turning the head, are capable of enduring weather, thirst, hunger, and over-abundance, and are blessed with stomachs which triumph over everything the wilderness may offer. Evidently their lives are not bitter.

The Grand Cañon of the Colorado

The largest of the cañon animals one is likely to see is the wild sheep, or Rocky Mountain bighorn, a most admirable beast, with limbs that never fail, at home on the most nerve-trying precipices, acquainted with all the springs and passes and broken-down jumpable places in the sheer ribbon cliffs, bounding from crag to crag in easy grace and confidence of strength, his great horns held high above his shoulders, wild red blood beating and hissing through every fiber of him like the wind through a quivering mountain pine.

Deer also are occasionally met in the cañon, making their way to the river when the wells of the plateau are dry. Along the short spring streams beavers are still busy, as is shown by the cottonwood and willow timber they have cut and peeled, found in all the river drift-heaps. In the most barren cliffs and gulches there dwell a multitude of lesser animals, well-dressed, clear-eyed, happy little beasts—wood-rats, kangaroo-rats, gophers, wood-mice, skunks, rabbits, bob cats, and many others, gathering food, or dozing in their sun-warmed dens. Lizards, too, of every kind and color are here enjoying life on the hot cliffs, and making the brightest of them brighter.

Nor is there any lack of feathered people. The golden eagle may be seen, and the osprey, hawks, jays, humming-birds, the mourning-dove, and cheery familiar singers—the black-headed grosbeak, robin, bluebird, Townsend's thrush, and many warblers, sailing the sky and enlivening the rocks and bushes through all the cañon wilderness.

Here at Hance's river camp or a few miles above it brave Powell and his brave men passed their first night in the cañon on their adventurous voyage of discovery thirty-three years ago. They faced a thousand dangers, open or hidden, now in their boats gladly sliding down swift, smooth reaches, now rolled over and over in back-combing surges of rough, roaring cataracts, sucked under in eddies, swimming like beavers, tossed and beaten like castaway drift—stout-hearted, undaunted, doing their work through it all. After a month of this they floated smoothly out of the dark, gloomy, roaring abyss into light and safety two hundred miles below. As the flood rushes past us, heavy-laden with desert mud, we naturally think of its sources, its countless silvery branches outspread on thousands of snowy mountains along the crest of the continent, and the life of them, the beauty of them, their history and romance. Its topmost springs are far north and east in Wyoming and Colorado, on the snowy Wind River, Front, Park, and Sawatch ranges, dividing the two ocean waters, and the Elk, Wasatch, Uinta, and innumerable spurs streaked with streams, made famous by early explorers and hunters. It is a river of rivers—the Du Chesne, San Rafael, Yampa, Dolores, Gunnison, Cotchetopa, Uncompahgre, Eagle, and Roaring rivers, the Green and the Grand, and scores of others with branches innumerable, as mad and glad a band as ever sang on mountains, descending in glory of foam and spray from snow-banks and glaciers through their rocky moraine-dammed, beaver-dammed channels. Then, all emerging from dark balsam and pine woods and coming together, they meander through wide, sunny park valleys, and at length enter the great plateau and flow in deep cañons, the beginning of the system culminating in this grand cañon of cañons.

Our warm cañon camp is also a good place to give a thought to

The Grand Cañon of the Colorado

the glaciers which still exist at the heads of the highest tributaries. Some of them are of considerable size, especially those on
the Wind River and Sawatch ranges in Wyoming and Colorado.
They are remnants of a vast system of glaciers which recently
covered the upper part of the Colorado basin, sculptured its
peaks, ridges, and valleys to their present forms, and extended
far out over the plateau region — how far I cannot now say. It appears, therefore, that, however old the main trunk of the Colorado may be, all its wide-spread upper branches and the landscapes they flow through are new-born, scarce at all changed as
yet in any important feature since they first came to light at the
close of the glacial period.

The so-called Grand Colorado Plateau, of which the Grand
Cañon is only one of its well-proportioned features, extends with
a breadth of hundreds of miles from the flanks of the Wasatch and
Park Mountains to the south of the San Francisco Peaks. Immediately to the north of the deepest part of the cañon it rises in a series of subordinate plateaus, diversified with green meadows,
marshes, bogs, ponds, forests, and grovy park valleys, a favorite
Indian hunting-ground, inhabited by elk, deer, beaver, etc. But
far the greater part of the plateau is good sound desert, rocky,
sandy, or fluffy with loose ashes and dust, dissected in some
places into a labyrinth of stream-channel chasms like cracks in a
dry clay-bed, or the narrow slit crevasses of glaciers, — black-
ened with lava-flows, dotted with volcanoes and beautiful buttes,
and lined with long continuous escarpments, — a vast bed of sediments of an ancient sea-bottom, still nearly as level as when first
laid down after being heaved into the sky a mile or two high.

John Muir

Walking quietly about in the alleys and byways of the Grand
Cañon City, we learn something of the way it was made; and all
must admire effects so great from means apparently so simple:
rain striking light hammer-blows or heavier in streams, with
many rest Sundays; soft air and light, gentle sappers and miners,
toiling forever; the big river sawing the plateau asunder, carrying away the eroded and ground waste, and exposing the edges of
the strata to the weather; rain torrents sawing cross-streets and
alleys, exposing the strata in the same way in hundreds of sections, the softer, less resisting beds weathering and receding
faster, thus undermining the harder beds, which fall, not only in
small weathered particles, but in heavy sheer-cleaving masses,
assisted down from time to time by kindly earthquakes, rain torrents rushing the fallen material to the river, keeping the wall
rocks constantly exposed. Thus the cañon grows wider and
deeper. So also do the side-cañons and amphitheaters, while secondary gorges and cirques gradually isolate masses of the promontories, forming new buildings, all of which are being weathered and pulled and shaken down while being built, showing
destruction and creation as one. We see the proudest temples and
palaces in stateliest attitudes, wearing their sheets of detritus as
royal robes, shedding off showers of red and yellow stones like
trees in autumn shedding their leaves, going to dust like beautiful
days to night, proclaiming as with the tongues of angels the natural beauty of death.

Every building is seen to be a remnant of once continuous
beds of sediments — sand and slime on the floor of an ancient sea,
and filled with the remains of animals, and that every particle of

The Grand Cañon of the Colorado

the sandstones and limestones of these wonderful structures was derived from other landscapes, weathered and rolled and ground in the storms and streams of other ages. And when we examine the escarpments, hills, buttes, and other monumental masses of the plateau on either side of the cañon, we discover that an amount of material has been carried off in the general denudation of the region compared with which even that carried away in the making of the Grand Cañon is as nothing. Thus each wonder in sight becomes a window through which other wonders come to view. In no other part of this continent are the wonders of geology, the records of the world's auld lang syne, more widely opened, or displayed in higher piles. The whole cañon is a mine of fossils, in which five thousand feet of horizontal strata are exposed in regular succession over more than a thousand square miles of wall-space, and on the adjacent plateau region there is another series of beds twice as thick, forming a grand geological library—a collection of stone books covering thousands of miles of shelving tier on tier conveniently arranged for the student. And with what wonderful scriptures are their pages filled—myriad forms of successive floras and faunas, lavishly illustrated with colored drawings, carrying us back into the midst of the life of a past infinitely remote. And as we go on and on, studying this old, old life in the light of the life beating warmly about us, we enrich and lengthen our own.

Travels in Alaska

*J*ohn Muir's trips to Alaska began in 1879 and continued in 1880, 1881, 1890, 1897, and 1899. His explorations in Alaska are a reprise of the solitary roamings and explorations that marked his younger life, and passages from his Alaskan journals have the same immediacy and intelligent enthusiasm as his earlier writing. More important, he was seeing what he had only speculated about—real "live" glaciers, one of which, the Muir Glacier, was named after him. Travels in Alaska was Muir's last book, completed from his notes and journals by a friend, Marion Randall Parsons. Because Muir had not finished all his planned editing, the last chapters are comprised of journal notations. The final section on auroras is one of the most charming pieces Muir ever wrote, a simple and direct response to a theatrical light show, and in it is the quintessence of Muir's love of light, life, and the natural world.

After we had passed through the Wrangell Narrows, the mountains of the mainland came in full view, gloriously arrayed in snow and ice, some of the largest and most river-like of the glaciers flowing through wide, high-walled valleys like Yosemite, their sources far back and concealed, others in plain sight, from their highest fountains to the level of the sea.

Cares of every kind were quickly forgotten, and though the Cassiar engines soon began to wheeze and sigh with doleful solemnity, suggesting coming trouble, we were too happy to mind them. Every face glowed with natural love of wild beauty. The islands were seen in long perspective, their forests dark green in the foreground, with varying tones of blue growing more and more tender in the distance; bays full of hazy shadows, graduating into open, silvery fields of light, and lofty headlands with fine arching insteps dipping their feet in the shining water. But every eye was turned to the mountains. Forgotten now were the Chilcats and missions while the word of God was being read in these majestic hieroglyphics blazoned along the sky. The earnest, childish wonderment with which this glorious page of Nature's Bible was contemplated was delightful to see. All evinced eager desire to learn.

"Is that a glacier," they asked, "down in that cañon? And is it all solid ice?"

"Yes."

"How deep is it?"

"Perhaps five hundred or a thousand feet."

"You say it flows. How can hard ice flow?"

"It flows like water, though invisibly slow."

"And where does it come from?"

"From snow that is heaped up every winter on the mountains."

"And how, then, is the snow changed into ice?"

"It is welded by the pressure of its own weight."

"Are these white masses we see in the hollows glaciers also?"

"Yes."

"Are those bluish draggled masses hanging down from beneath the snow-fields what you call the snouts of the glaciers?"

"Yes."

"What made the hollows they are in?"

Travels in Alaska

"The glaciers themselves, just as traveling animals make their own tracks."

"How long have they been there?"

"Numberless centuries," etc. I answered as best I could, keeping up a running commentary on the subject in general, while busily engaged in sketching and noting my own observations, preaching glacial gospel in a rambling way, while the Cassiar, slowly wheezing and creeping along the shore, shifted our position so that the icy cañons were opened to view and closed again in regular succession, like the leaves of a book [pp. 56–58].

Standing in the gateway of this glorious temple, and regarding it only as a picture, its outlines may be easily traced, the water foreground of a pale-green color, a smooth mirror sheet sweeping back five or six miles like one of the lower reaches of a great river, bounded at the head by a beveled barrier wall of bluish-white ice four or five hundred feet high. A few snowy mountain-tops appear beyond it, and on either hand rise a series of majestic, pale-gray granite rocks from three to four thousand feet high, some of them thinly forested and striped with bushes and flowery grass on narrow shelves, especially about half way up, others severely sheer and bare and built together into walls like those of Yosemite, extending far beyond the ice barrier, one immense brow appearing beyond another with their bases buried in the glacier. This is a Yosemite Valley in process of formation, the modeling and sculpture of the walls nearly completed and well planted, but no groves as yet or gardens or meadows on the raw and unfinished bottom. It is as if the explorer, in entering the Merced Yosemite, should find the walls nearly in their present condition, trees and flowers in the warm nooks and along the sunny portions of the moraine-covered brows, but the bottom of the valley still covered with water and beds of gravel and mud, and the grand glacier that formed it slowly receding but still filling the upper half of the valley [pp. 64–65].

The whole front of the glacier is gashed and sculptured into a maze of shallow caves and crevasses, and a bewildering variety of novel architectural forms, clusters of glittering lance-tipped spires, gables, and obelisks, bold outstanding bastions and plain mural cliffs, adorned along the top with fretted cornice and battlement, while every gorge and crevasse, groove and hollow, was filled with light, shimmering and throbbing in pale-blue tones of ineffable tenderness and beauty. The day was warm, and back on the broad melting bosom of the glacier beyond the crevassed front, many streams were rejoicing, gurgling, ringing, singing, in frictionless channels worn down through the white disintegrated ice of the surface into the quick and living blue, in which they flowed with a grace of motion and flashing of light to be found only on the crystal hillocks and ravines of a glacier.

Along the sides of the glacier we saw the mighty flood grinding against the granite walls with tremendous pressure, rounding outswelling bosses, and deepening the retreating hollows into the forms they are destined to have when, in the fullness of appointed time, the huge ice tool shall be withdrawn by the sun. Every feature glowed with intention, reflecting the plans of God. Back a few miles from the front, the glacier is now probably but little more than a thousand feet deep; but when we examine the records on the walls, the rounded, grooved, striated, and polished features so surely glacial, we learn that in the earlier days of the ice age they were all over-swept, and that this glacier has flowed at a height of from three to four thousand feet above its present level, when it was at least a mile deep.

Standing here, with facts so fresh and telling and held up so vividly before us, every seeing observer, not to say geologist, must readily apprehend the earth-sculpturing, landscape-making action of flowing ice. And here, too, one learns that the world, though made, is yet being made; that this is still the morning of creation; that mountains long conceived are now being born, channels traced for coming rivers, basins hollowed for lakes; that moraine soil is being ground and outspread for coming plants, — coarse boulders and gravel for forests, finer soil for grasses and flowers, — while the finest part of the grist, seen hastening out to sea in the draining streams, is being stored away in darkness and builded particle on particle, cementing and crystallizing, to make the mountains and valleys and plains of other predestined landscapes, to be followed by still others in endless rhythm and beauty [pp. 66–68].

The carved totem-pole monuments are the most striking of the objects displayed here. The simplest of them consisted of a smooth, round post fifteen or twenty feet high and about eighteen inches in diameter, with the figure of some animal on top — a bear, porpoise, eagle, or raven, about life-size or larger. These were the totems of the families that occupied the houses in front of which they stood. Others supported the figure of a man or woman, life-size or larger, usually in a sitting posture, said to resemble the dead whose ashes were contained in a closed cavity in the pole. The largest were thirty or forty feet high, carved from top to bottom into human and animal totem figures, one above another, with their limbs grotesquely doubled and folded. Some of the most imposing were said to commemorate some event of an historical character. But a telling display of family pride seemed to have been the prevailing motive. All the figures were more or less rude, and some were broadly grotesque, but there was never any feebleness or obscurity in the expression. On the contrary, every feature showed grave force and decision; while the childish audacity displayed in the designs, combined with manly strength in their execution, was truly wonderful.

The colored lichens and mosses gave them a venerable air, while the larger vegetation often found on such as were most decayed produced a picturesque effect. Here, for example, is a bear five or six feet long, reposing on top of his lichen-clad pillar, with paws comfortably folded, a tuft of grass growing in each ear and rubus bushes along his back. And yonder is an old chief poised on a taller pillar, apparently gazing out over the landscape in contemplative mood, a tuft of bushes leaning back with a jaunty air from the top of his weatherbeaten hat, and downy mosses about his massive lips. But no rudeness or grotesqueness that may appear, however combined with the decorations that nature has added, may possibly provoke mirth. The whole work is serious in aspect and brave and true in execution.

Similar monuments are made by other Thlinkit tribes. The erection of a totem pole is made a grand affair, and is often talked of for a year or two beforehand. A feast, to which many are invited, is held, and the joyous occasion is spent in eating, dancing, and the distribution of gifts. Some of the larger specimens cost a thousand dollars or more. From one to two hundred blankets, worth three dollars apiece, are paid to the genius who carves them, while the presents and feast usually cost twice as much, so that only the wealthy families can afford them. I talked with an old Indian who pointed out one of the carvings he had made in the Wrangell village, for which he told me he had received forty blankets, a gun, a canoe, and other articles, all together worth about $170 [pp. 72–74].

Next morning I set out from Glenora to climb Glenora Peak for the general view of the great Coast Range that I failed to obtain on my first ascent on account of the accident that befell Mr. Young when we were within a minute or two of the top. It is hard to fail in reaching a mountain-top that one starts for, let the cause be what it may. This time I had no companion to care for, but the sky was threatening. I was assured by the local weather-prophets that the day would be rainy or snowy because the peaks in sight were muffled in clouds that seemed to be getting ready for work. I determined to go ahead, however, for storms of any kind are well worth while, and if driven back I could wait and try again.

With crackers in my pocket and a light rubber coat that a kind Hebrew passenger on the steamer Gertrude loaned me, I was ready for anything that might offer, my hopes for the grand view rising and falling as the clouds rose and fell. Anxiously I watched them as they trailed their draggled skirts across the glaciers and fountain peaks as if thoughtfully looking for the places where they could do the most good. From Glenora there is first a terrace two hundred feet above the river covered mostly with bushes, yellow apocynum on the open spaces, together with carpets of dwarf manzanita, bunch-grass, and a few of the compositæ, galiums, etc. Then comes a flat stretch a mile wide, extending to the foothills, covered with birch, spruce, fir, and poplar, now mostly killed by fire and the ground strewn with charred trunks. From this black forest the mountain rises in rather steep slopes covered with a luxuriant growth of bushes, grass, flowers, and a few trees, chiefly spruce and fir, the firs gradually dwarfing into a beautiful chaparral, the most beautiful, I think, I have ever seen, the flat fan-shaped plumes thickly foliaged and imbricated by snow pressure, forming a smooth, handsome thatch which bears cones and thrives as if this repressed condition were its very best. It extends up to an elevation of about fifty-five hundred feet. Only a few trees more than a foot in diameter and more than fifty feet high are found higher than four thousand feet above the sea. A few poplars and willows occur on moist places, gradually dwarfing like the conifers. Alder is the most generally distributed of the chaparral bushes, growing nearly everywhere; its crinkled stems an inch or two thick form a troublesome tangle to the mountaineer. The blue geranium, with leaves red and showy at this time of the year, is perhaps the most telling of the flowering plants. It grows up to five thousand feet or more. Larkspurs are common, with epilobium, senecio, erigeron, and a few solidagos. The harebell appears at about four thousand feet and extends to the summit, dwarfing in stature but maintaining the size of its handsome bells until they seem to be lying loose and detached on the ground as if like snow flowers they had fallen from the sky; and, though frail and delicate-looking, none of its companions is more enduring or rings out the praises of beauty-loving Nature in tones more appreciable to mortals, not forgetting even Cassiope, who also is here and her companion, Bryanthus, the loveliest and most widely distributed of the alpine shrubs. Then come crowberry, and two species of huckleberry, one of them from about six inches to a foot high with delicious berries, the other a most lavishly prolific and contented-looking dwarf, few of the bushes being more than two inches high, counting to the topmost leaf, yet each bearing from ten to twenty or more large berries. Perhaps more than half the bulk of the whole plant is fruit, the largest and finest-flavored of all the huckleberries or blueberries I ever tasted, spreading fine feasts for the grouse and ptarmigan and many others of Nature's mountain people. I noticed three species of dwarf willows, one with narrow leaves, growing at the very summit of the mountain in cracks of the rocks, as well as on patches of soil, another with large, smooth leaves now turning yellow. The third species grows between the others as to elevation; its leaves, then orange-colored, are strikingly pitted and reticulated. Another alpine shrub, a species of sericocarpus, covered with handsome heads of feathery achenia, beautiful dwarf echiverias with flocks of purple flowers pricked into their bright grass-green, cushion-like bosses of moss-like foliage, and a fine forget-me-not reach to the summit. I may also mention a large mertensia, a fine anemone, a veratrum, six feet high, a large blue daisy, growing up to three to four thousand feet, and at the summit a dwarf species, with dusky, hairy involucres, and a few ferns, aspidium, gymnogramma, and small rock cheilanthes, leaving scarce a foot of ground bare, though the mountain looks bald and brown in the distance like those of the desert ranges of the Great Basin in Utah and Nevada.

Charmed with these plant people, I had almost forgotten to watch the sky until I reached the top of the highest peak, when one of the greatest and most impressively sublime of all the mountain views I have ever enjoyed came full in sight — more than three hundred miles of closely packed peaks of the great Coast Range, sculptured in the boldest manner imaginable, their naked tops and dividing ridges dark in color, their sides and the cañons, gorges, and valleys between them loaded with glaciers and snow. From this standpoint I counted upwards of two hundred glaciers, while dark-centred luminous clouds with fringed edges hovered and crawled over them, now slowly descending, casting transparent shadows on the ice and snow, now rising high above them, lingering like loving angels guarding the crystal gifts they had bestowed. Although the range as seen from this Glenora mountain-top seems regular in its trend, as if the main axis were simple and continuous, it is, on the contrary, far from simple. In front of the highest ranks of peaks are others of the same form with their own glaciers, and lower peaks before these, and yet lower ones with their ridges and cañons, valleys and foothills. Alps rise beyond alps as far as the eye can reach, and clusters of higher peaks here and there closely crowded together; clusters, too, of needles and pinnacles innumerable like trees in groves. Everywhere the peaks seem comparatively slender and closely packed, as if Nature had here been trying to see how many noble well-dressed mountains could be crowded into one grand range.

The black rocks, too steep for snow to lie upon, were brought into sharp relief by white clouds and snow and glaciers, and these again were outlined and made tellingly plain by the rocks. The glaciers so grandly displayed are of every form, some crawling through gorge and valley like monster glittering serpents; others like broad cataracts pouring over cliffs into shadowy gulfs; others, with their main trunks winding through narrow cañons, display long, white finger-like tributaries descending from the summits of pinnacled ridges. Others lie back in fountain cirques walled in all around save at the lower edge, over which they pour in blue cascades. Snow, too, lay in folds and patches of every form on blunt, rounded ridges in curves, arrowy lines, dashes, and narrow ornamental flutings among the summit peaks and in broad radiating wings on smooth slopes. And on many a bulging headland and lower ridge there lay heavy, over-curling copings and smooth, white domes where wind-driven snow was pressed and wreathed and packed into every form and in every possible place and condition. I never before had seen so richly sculptured a range or so many awe-inspiring inaccessible mountains crowded together. If a line were drawn east and west from the peak on which I stood, and extended both ways to the horizon, cutting the whole round landscape in two equal parts, then all of the south half would be bounded by these icy peaks, which would seem to curve around half the horizon and about twenty degrees more, though extending in a general straight, or but moderately curved, line. The deepest and thickest and highest of all this wilderness of peaks lie to the southwest. They are probably from about nine to twelve thousand feet high, springing to this elevation from near the sea-level. The peak on which these observations were made is somewhere about seven thousand feet high, and from here I estimated the height of the range. The highest peak of all, or that seemed so to me, lies to the westward at an estimated distance of about one hundred and fifty or two hundred miles. Only its solid white summit was visible. Possibly it may be the topmost peak of St. Elias. Now look northward around the other half of the horizon, and instead of countless peaks crowding into the sky, you see a low brown region, heaving and swelling in gentle curves, apparently scarcely more waved than a rolling prairie. The so-called cañons of several forks of the upper Stickeen are visible, but even where best seen in the foreground and middle ground of the picture, they are like mere sunken gorges, making scarce perceptible marks on the landscape, while the tops of the highest mountain-swells show only small patches of snow and no glaciers.

Glenora Peak, on which I stood, is the highest point of a spur that puts out from the main range in a northerly direction. It seems to have been a rounded, broad-backed ridge which has been sculptured into its present irregular form by short residual glaciers, some of which, a mile or two long, are still at work.

As I lingered, gazing on the vast show, luminous shadowy clouds seemed to increase in glory of color and motion, now fondling the highest peaks with infinite tenderness of touch, now hovering above them like eagles over their nests.

When night was drawing near, I ran down the flowery slopes exhilarated, thanking God for the gift of this great day. The setting sun fired the clouds. All the world seemed new-born. Every thing, even the commonest, was seen in new light and was looked at with new interest as if never seen before. The plant people seemed glad, as if rejoicing with me, the little ones as well as the trees, while every feature of the peak and its traveled boulders seemed to know what I had been about and the depth of my joy, as if they could read faces [pp. 90–96].

Next day I planned an excursion to the so-called Dirt Glacier, the most interesting to Indians and steamer men of all the Stickeen glaciers from its mysterious floods. I left the steamer Gertrude for the glacier delta an hour or two before sunset. The captain kindly loaned me his canoe and two of his Indian deck hands, who seemed much puzzled to know what the rare service required of them might mean, and on leaving bade a merry adieu to their companions. We camped on the west side of the river opposite the front of the glacier, in a spacious valley surrounded by snowy mountains. Thirteen small glaciers were in sight and four waterfalls. It was a fine, serene evening, and the highest peaks were wearing turbans of flossy, gossamer cloud-stuff. I had my supper before leaving the steamer, so I had only to make a camp-fire, spread my blanket, and lie down. The Indians had their own bedding and lay beside their own fire.

The Dirt Glacier is noted among the river men as being subject to violent flood outbursts once or twice a year, usually in the late summer. The delta of this glacier stream is three or four miles wide where it fronts the river, and the many rough channels with which it is guttered and the uprooted trees and huge boulders that roughen its surface manifest the power of the floods that swept them to their places; but under ordinary conditions the glacier discharges its drainage water into the river through only four or five of the delta-channels.

Our camp was made on the south or lower side of the delta, below all the draining streams, so that I would not have to ford any of them on my way to the glacier. The Indians chose a sand-pit to sleep in; I chose a level spot back of a drift log. I had but little to say to my companions as they could speak no English, nor I much Thlinkit or Chinook. In a few minutes after landing they retired to their pit and were soon asleep and asnore. I lingered by the fire until after ten o'clock, for the night sky was clear, and the great white mountains in the starlight seemed nearer than by day and to be looking down like guardians of the valley, while the water-falls, and the torrents escaping from beneath the big glacier, roared in a broad, low monotone, sounding as if close at hand, though, as it proved next day, the nearest was three miles away. After wrapping myself in my blankets, I still gazed into the marvelous sky and made out to sleep only about two hours. Then, without waking the noisy sleepers, I arose, ate a piece of bread, and set out in my shirt-sleeves, determined to make the most of the time at my disposal. The captain was to pick us up about noon at a woodpile about a mile from here; but if in the mean time the steamer should run aground and he should need his canoe, a three-whistle signal would be given.

Following a dry channel for about a mile, I came suddenly upon the main outlet of the glacier, which in the imperfect light seemed as large as the river, about one hundred and fifty feet wide, and perhaps three or four feet deep. A little farther up it was only about fifty feet wide and rushing on with impetuous roaring force in its rocky channel, sweeping forward sand, gravel, cobblestones, and boulders, the bump and rumble sounds of the largest of these rolling stones being readily heard in the midst of the roaring. It was too swift and tough to ford, and no bridge tree could be found, for the great floods had cleared everything out of their way. I was therefore compelled to keep on up the right bank, however difficult the way. Where a strip of bare boulders lined the margin, the walking was easy, but where the current swept close along the ragged edge of the forest, progress was difficult and slow on account of snow-crinkled and interlaced thickets of alder and willow, reinforced with fallen trees and thorny devil's-club (*Echinopanax horridum*), making a jungle all but impenetrable. The mile of this extravagantly difficult growth through which I struggled, inch by inch, will not soon be forgotten. At length arriving within a few hundred yards of the glacier, full of panax barbs, I found that both the glacier and its unfordable stream were pressing hard against a shelving cliff, dangerously steep, leaving no margin, and compelling me to scramble along its face before I could get on to the glacier. But by sunrise all these cliff, jungle, and torrent troubles were overcome and I gladly found myself free on the magnificent ice-river.

The curving, out-bulging front of the glacier is about two miles wide, two hundred feet high, and its surface for a mile or so above the front is strewn with moraine detritus, giving it a strangely dirty, dusky look, hence its name, the "Dirt Glacier," this detritus-laden portion being all that is seen in passing up the river. A mile or two beyond the moraine-covered part I was surprised to find alpine plants growing on the ice, fresh and green, some of them in full flower. These curious glacier gardens, the first I had seen, were evidently planted by snow avalanches from the high walls. They were well watered, of course, by the melting surface of the ice and fairly well nourished by humus still attached to the roots, and in some places formed beds of considerable thickness. Seedling trees and bushes also were growing among the flowers. Admiring these novel floating gardens, I struck out for the middle of the pure white glacier, where the ice seemed smoother, and then held straight on for about eight miles, where I reluctantly turned back to meet the steamer, greatly regretting that I had not brought a week's supply of hardtack to allow me to explore the glacier to its head, and then trust to some passing canoe to take me down to Buck Station, from which I could explore the Big Stickeen Glacier.

Travels in Alaska

Altogether, I saw about fifteen or sixteen miles of the main trunk. The grade is almost regular, and the walls on either hand are about from two to three thousand feet high, sculptured like those of Yosemite Valley. I found no difficulty of an extraordinary kind. Many a crevasse had to be crossed, but most of them were narrow and easily jumped, while the few wide ones that lay in my way were crossed on sliver bridges or avoided by passing around them. The structure of the glacier was strikingly revealed on its melting surface. It is made up of thin vertical or inclined sheets or slabs set on edge and welded together. They represent, I think, the successive snowfalls from heavy storms on the tributaries. One of the tributaries on the right side, about three miles above the front, has been entirely melted off from the trunk and has receded two or three miles, forming an independent glacier. Across the mouth of this abandoned part of its channel the main glacier flows, forming a dam which gives rise to a lake. On the head of the detached tributary there are some five or six small residual glaciers, the drainage of which, with that of the snowy mountain slopes above them, discharges into the lake, whose outlet is through a channel or channels beneath the damming glacier. Now these sub-channels are occasionally blocked and the water rises until it flows alongside of the glacier, but as the dam is a moving one, a grand outburst is sometimes made, which, draining the large lake, produces a flood of amazing power, sweeping down immense quantities of moraine material and raising the river all the way down to its mouth, so that several trips may occasionally be made by the steamers after the season of low water has laid them up for the year. The occurrence of these floods are, of course, well known to the Indians and steamboat men, though they know nothing of their cause. They simply remark, "The Dirt Glacier has broken out again."

I greatly enjoyed my walk up this majestic ice-river, charmed by the pale-blue, ineffably fine light in the crevasses, moulins, and wells, and the innumerable azure pools in basins of azure ice, and the network of surface streams, large and small, gliding, swirling with wonderful grace of motion in their frictionless channels, calling forth devout admiration at almost every step and filling the mind with a sense of Nature's endless beauty and power. Looking ahead from the middle of the glacier, you see the broad white flood, though apparently rigid as iron, sweeping in graceful curves between its high mountain-like walls, small glaciers hanging in the hollows on either side, and snow in every form above them, and the great down-plunging granite buttresses and headlands of the walls marvelous in bold massive sculpture; forests in side cañons to within fifty feet of the glacier; avalanche pathways overgrown with alder and willow; innumerable cascades keeping up a solemn harmony of water sounds blending with those of the glacier moulins and rills; and as far as the eye can reach, tributary glaciers at short intervals silently descending from their high, white fountains to swell the grand central ice-river.

In the angle formed by the main glacier and the lake that gives rise to the river floods, there is a massive granite dome sparsely feathered with trees, and just beyond this yosemitic rock is a mountain, perhaps ten thousand feet high, laden with ice and snow which seemed pure pearly white in the morning light. Last evening as seen from camp it was adorned with a cloud streamer, and both the streamer and the peak were flushed in the alpenglow. A mile or two above this mountain, on the opposite side of the glacier, there is a rock like the Yosemite Sentinel; and in general all the wall rocks as far as I saw them are more or less yosemitic in form and color and streaked with cascades.

But wonderful as this noble ice-river is in size and depth and in power displayed, far more wonderful was the vastly greater glacier three or four thousand feet, or perhaps a mile, in depth, whose size and general history is inscribed on the sides of the walls and over the tops of the rocks in characters which have not yet been greatly dimmed by the weather. Comparing its present size with that when it was in its prime, is like comparing a small rivulet to the same stream when it is a roaring torrent.

The return trip to the camp past the shelving cliff and through the weary devil's-club jungle was made in a few hours. The Indians had gone off picking berries, but were on the watch for me and hailed me as I approached. The captain had called for me, and, after waiting three hours, departed for Wrangell without leaving any food, to make sure, I suppose, of a quick return of his Indians and canoe. This was no serious matter, however, for the swift current swept us down to Buck Station, some thirty-five miles distant, by eight o'clock. Here I remained to study the "Big Stickeen Glacier," but the Indians set out for Wrangell soon after supper, though I invited them to stay till morning.

The weather that morning, August 27, was dark and rainy, and I tried to persuade myself that I ought to rest a day before setting out on new ice work. But just across the river the "Big Glacier" was staring me in the face, pouring its majestic flood through a broad mountain gateway and expanding in the spacious river valley to a width of four or five miles, while dim in the gray distance loomed its high mountain fountains. So grand an invitation displayed in characters so telling was of course irresistible, and body-care and weather-care vanished.

Mr. Choquette, the keeper of the station, ferried me across the river, and I spent the day in getting general views and planning the work that had been long in mind. I first traced the broad, complicated terminal moraine to its southern extremity, climbed up the west side along the lateral moraine three or four miles, making my way now on the glacier, now on the moraine-covered bank, and now compelled to climb up through the timber and brush in order to pass some rocky headland, until I reached a point commanding a good general view of the lower end of the glacier. Heavy, blotting rain then began to fall, and I retraced my steps, oftentimes stopping to admire the blue ice-caves into which glad, rejoicing streams from the mountain-side were hurrying as if going home, while the glacier seemed to open wide its crystal gateways to welcome them.

The following morning blotting rain was still falling, but time and work was too precious to mind it. Kind Mr. Choquette put me across the river in a canoe, with a lot of biscuits his Indian wife had baked for me and some dried salmon, a little sugar and tea, a blanket, and a piece of light sheeting for shelter from rain during the night, all rolled into one bundle.

"When shall I expect you back?" inquired Choquette, when I bade him good-bye.

Travels in Alaska

"Oh, any time," I replied. "I shall see as much as possible of the glacier, and I know not how long it will hold me."

"Well, but when will I come to look for you, if anything happens? Where are you going to try to go? Years ago Russian officers from Sitka went up the glacier from here and none ever returned. It's a mighty dangerous glacier, all full of damn deep holes and cracks. You've no idea what ticklish deceiving traps are scattered over it."

"Yes, I have," I said. "I have seen glaciers before, though none so big as this one. Do not look for me until I make my appearance on the river-bank. Never mind me. I am used to caring for myself." And so, shouldering my bundle, I trudged off through the moraine boulders and thickets.

My general plan was to trace the terminal moraine to its extreme north end, pitch my little tent, leave the blanket and most of the hardtack, and from this main camp go and come as hunger required or allowed.

After examining a cross-section of the broad moraine, roughened by concentric masses, marking interruptions in the recession of the glacier of perhaps several centuries, in which the successive moraines were formed and shoved together in closer or wider order, I traced the moraine to its northeastern extremity and ascended the glacier for several miles along the left margin, then crossed it at the grand cataract and down the right side to the river, and along the moraine to the point of beginning.

On the older portions of this moraine I discovered several kettles in process of formation and was pleased to find that they conformed in the most striking way with the theory I had already been led to make from observations on the old kettles which form so curious a feature of the drift covering Wisconsin and Minnesota and some of the larger moraines of the residual glaciers in the California Sierra. I found a pit eight or ten feet deep with raw shifting sides countersunk abruptly in the rough moraine material, and at the bottom, on sliding down by the aid of a lithe spruce tree that was being undermined, I discovered, after digging down a foot or two, that the bottom was resting on a block of solid blue ice which had been buried in the moraine perhaps a century or more, judging by the age of the tree that had grown above it. Probably more than another century will be required to complete the formation of this kettle by the slow melting of the buried ice-block. The moraine material of course was falling in as the ice melted, and the sides maintained an angle as steep as the material would lie. All sorts of theories have been advanced for the formation of these kettles, so abundant in the drift over a great part of the United States, and I was glad to be able to set the question at rest, at least as far as I was concerned.

The glacier and the mountains about it are on so grand a scale and so generally inaccessible in the ordinary sense, it seemed to matter but little what course I pursued. Everything was full of interest, even the weather, though about as unfavorable as possible for wide views, and scrambling through the moraine jungle brush kept one as wet as if all the way was beneath a cascade.

I pushed on, with many a rest and halt to admire the bold and marvelously sculptured ice-front, looking all the grander and more striking in the gray mist with all the rest of the glacier shut out, until I came to a lake about two hundred yards wide and two miles long with scores of small bergs floating in it, some aground, close inshore against the moraine, the light playing on their angles and shimmering in their blue caves in ravishing tones. This proved to be the largest of the series of narrow lakelets that lie in shallow troughs between the moraine and the glacier, a miniature Arctic Ocean, its ice-cliffs played upon by whispering, rippling wavelets and its small berg floes drifting in its currents or with the wind, or stranded here and there along its rocky moraine shore.

Hundreds of small rills and good-sized streams were falling into the lake from the glacier, singing in low tones, some of them pouring in sheer falls over blue cliffs from narrow ice-valleys, some spouting from pipelike channels in the solid front of the glacier, others gurgling out of arched openings at the base. All these water-streams were riding on the parent ice-stream, their voices joined in one grand anthem telling the wonders of their near and far-off fountains. The lake itself is resting in a basin of ice, and the forested moraine, though seemingly cut off from the glacier and probably more than a century old, is in great part resting on buried ice left behind as the glacier receded, and melting slowly on account of the protection afforded by the moraine detritus, which keeps shifting and falling on the inner face long after it is overgrown with lichens, mosses, grasses, bushes, and even good-sized trees; these changes going on with marvelous deliberation until in fullness of time the whole moraine settles down upon its bedrock foundation.

The outlet of the lake is a large stream, almost a river in size, one of the main draining streams of the glacier. I attempted to ford it where it begins to break in rapids in passing over the moraine, but found it too deep and rough on the bottom. I then tried to ford at its head, where it is wider and glides smoothly out of the lake, bracing myself against the current with a pole, but found it too deep, and when the icy water reached my shoulders I cautiously struggled back to the moraine. I next followed it down through the rocky jungle to a place where in breaking across the moraine dam it was only about thirty-five feet wide. Here I found a spruce tree, which I felled for a bridge; it reached across, about ten feet of the top holding in the bank brush. But the force of the torrent, acting on the submerged branches and the slender end of the trunk, bent it like a bow and made it very unsteady, and after testing it by going out about a third of the way over, it seemed likely to be carried away when bent deeper into the current by my weight. Fortunately, I discovered another larger tree well situated a little farther down, which I felled, and though a few feet in the middle was submerged, it seemed perfectly safe.

As it was now getting late, I started back to the lakeside where I had left my bundle, and in trying to hold a direct course found the interlaced jungle still more difficult than it was along the bank of the torrent. For over an hour I had to creep and struggle close to the rocky ground like a fly in a spider-web without being able to obtain a single glimpse of any guiding feature of the landscape. Finding a little willow taller than the surrounding alders, I climbed it, caught sight of the glacier-front, took a compass bearing, and sunk again into the dripping, blinding maze of brush, and at length emerged on the lakeshore seven hours after leaving it, all this time as wet as though I had been swimming, thus completing a trying day's work. But everything was deliciously fresh, and I found new and old plant friends, and lessons on Nature's Alaska moraine landscape-gardening that made everything bright and light.

It was now near dark, and I made haste to make up my flimsy little tent. The ground was desperately rocky. I made out, however, to level down a strip large enough to lie on, and by means of slim alder stems bent over it and tied together soon had a home. While thus busily engaged I was startled by a thundering roar across the lake. Running to the top of the moraine, I discovered that the tremendous noise was only the outcry of a newborn berg about fifty or sixty feet in diameter, rocking and wallowing in the waves it had raised as if enjoying its freedom after its long grinding work as part of the glacier. After this fine last lesson I managed to make a small fire out of wet twigs, got a cup of tea, stripped off my dripping clothing, wrapped myself in a blanket and lay brooding on the gains of the day and plans for the morrow, glad, rich, and almost comfortable.

It was raining hard when I awoke, but I made up my mind to disregard the weather, put on my dripping clothing, glad to know it was fresh and clean; ate biscuits and a piece of dried salmon without attempting to make a tea fire; filled a bag with hardtack, slung it over my shoulder, and with my indispensable ice-axe plunged once more into the dripping jungle. I found my bridge holding bravely in place against the swollen torrent, crossed it and beat my way around pools and logs and through two hours of tangle back to the moraine on the north side of the outlet, — a wet, weary battle but not without enjoyment. The smell of the washed ground and vegetation made every breath a pleasure, and I found *Calypso borealis*, the first I had seen on this side of the continent, one of my darlings, worth any amount of hardship; and I saw one of my Douglas squirrels on the margin of a grassy pool. The drip of the rain on the various leaves was pleasant to hear. More especially marked were the flat low-toned bumps and splashes of large drops from the trees on the broad horizontal leaves of *Echinopanax horridum*, like the drumming of thunder-shower drops on veratrum and palm leaves, while the mosses were indescribably beautiful, so fresh, so bright, so cheerily green, and all so low and calm and silent, however heavy and wild the wind and the rain blowing and pouring above them. Surely never a particle of dust has touched leaf or crown of all these blessed mosses; and how bright were the red rims of the cladonia cups beside them, and the fruit of the dwarf cornel! And the wet berries, Nature's precious jewelry, how beautiful they were! — huckleberries with pale bloom and a crystal drop on each; red and yellow salmon-berries, with clusters of smaller drops; and the glittering, berry-like raindrops adorning the interlacing arches of bent grasses and sedges around the edges of the pools, every drop a mirror with all the landscape in it. A' that and a' that and twice as muckle's a' that in this glorious Alaska day, recalling, however different, George Herbert's "Sweet day, so cool, so calm, so bright."

In the gardens and forests of this wonderful moraine one might spend a whole joyful life.

When I at last reached the end of the great moraine and the front of the mountain that forms the north side of the glacier basin, I tried to make my way along its side, but, finding the climbing tedious and difficult, took to the glacier and fared well, though a good deal of step-cutting was required on its ragged, crevassed margin. When night was drawing nigh, I scanned the steep mountainside in search of an accessible bench, however narrow, where a bed and a fire might be gathered for a camp. About dark great was my delight to find a little shelf with a few small mountain hemlocks growing in cleavage joints. Projecting knobs below it enabled me to build a platform for a fireplace and a bed, and by industrious creeping from one fissure to another, cutting bushes and small trees and sliding them down to within reach of my rock-shelf, I made out to collect wood enough to last through the night. In an hour or two I had a cheery fire, and spent the night in turning from side to side, steaming and drying after being wet two days and a night. Fortunately this night it did not rain, but it was very cold.

Pushing on next day, I climbed to the top of the glacier by ice-steps and along its side to the grand cataract two miles wide where the whole majestic flood of the glacier pours like a mighty surging river down a steep declivity in its channel. After gazing a long time on the glorious show, I discovered a place beneath the edge of the cataract where it flows over a hard, resisting granite rib, into which I crawled and enjoyed the novel and instructive view of a glacier pouring over my head, showing not only its grinding, polishing action, but how it breaks off large angular boulder-masses — a most telling lesson in earth-sculpture, confirming many I had already learned in the glacier basins of the

John Muir

High Sierra of California. I then crossed to the south side, noting the forms of the huge blocks into which the glacier was broken in passing over the brow of the cataract, and how they were welded.

The weather was now clear, opening views according to my own heart far into the high snowy mountains. I saw what seemed the farthest mountains, perhaps thirty miles from the front, everywhere winter-bound, but thick forested, however steep, for a distance of at least fifteen miles from the front, the trees, hemlock and spruce, clinging to the rock by root-holds among cleavage joints. The greatest discovery was in methods of denudation displayed beneath the glacier.

After a few more days of exhilarating study I returned to the river-bank opposite Choquette's landing. Promptly at sight of the signal I made, the kind Frenchman came across for me in his canoe. At his house I enjoyed a rest while writing out notes; then examined the smaller glacier fronting the one I had been exploring, until a passing canoe bound for Fort Wrangell took me aboard [pp. 97–113].

In the evening, after witnessing the unveiling of the majestic peaks and glaciers and their baptism in the down-pouring sunbeams, it seemed inconceivable that nature could have anything finer to show us. Nevertheless, compared with what was to come the next morning, all that was as nothing. The calm dawn gave no promise of anything uncommon. Its most impressive features were the frosty clearness of the sky and a deep, brooding stillness made all the more striking by the thunder of the newborn bergs. The sunrise we did not see at all, for we were beneath the shadows of the fiord cliffs; but in the midst of our studies, while the Indians were getting ready to sail, we were startled by the sudden appearance of a red light burning with a strange unearthly splendor on the topmost peak of the Fairweather Mountains. Instead of vanishing as suddenly as it had appeared, it spread and spread until the whole range down to the level of the glaciers was filled with the celestial fire. In color it was at first a vivid crimson, with a thick, furred appearance, as fine as the alpenglow, yet indescribably rich and deep — not in the least like a garment or mere external flush or bloom through which one might expect to see the rocks or snow, but every mountain apparently was glowing from the heart like molten metal fresh from a furnace. Beneath the frosty shadows of the fiord we stood hushed and awe-stricken, gazing at the holy vision; and had we seen the heavens opened and God made manifest, our attention could not have been more tremendously strained. When the highest peak began to burn, it did not seem to be steeped in sunshine, however glorious, but rather as if it had been thrust into the body of the sun itself. Then the supernal fire slowly descended, with a sharp line of demarkation separating it from the the cold, shaded region beneath; peak after peak, with their spires and ridges and cascading glaciers, caught the heavenly glow, until all the mighty host stood transfigured, hushed, and thoughtful, as if awaiting the coming of the Lord. The white, rayless light of morning, seen when I was alone amid the peaks of the California Sierra, had always seemed to me the most telling of all the terrestrial manifestations of God. But here the mountains themselves were made divine, and declared His glory in terms still more impressive. How long we gazed I never knew. The glorious vision passed away in a gradual, fading change through a thousand tones of color to pale yellow and white, and then the work of the ice-world went on again in everyday beauty. The green waters of the fiord were filled with sun-spangles; the fleet of icebergs set forth on their voyages with the upspringing breeze; and on the innumerable mirrors and prisms of these bergs, and on those of the shattered crystal walls of the glaciers, common white light and rainbow light began to burn, while the mountains shone in their frosty jewelry, and loomed again in the thin azure in serene terrestrial majesty. We turned and sailed away, joining the outgoing bergs, while "Gloria in excelsis" still seemed to be sounding over all the white landscape, and our burning hearts were ready for any fate, feeling that, whatever the future might have in store, the treasures we had gained this glorious morning would enrich our lives forever [pp. 152–54].

On our way down the coast, after examining the front of the beautiful Geikie Glacier, we obtained our first broad view of the great glacier afterwards named the Muir, the last of all the grand company to be seen, the stormy weather having hidden it when we first entered the bay. It was now perfectly clear, and the spacious, prairie-like glacier, with its many tributaries extending far back into the snowy recesses of its fountains, made a magnificent display of its wealth, and I was strongly tempted to go and explore it at all hazards. But winter had come, and the freezing of its fiords was an insurmountable obstacle. I had, therefore, to be content for the present with sketching and studying its main features at a distance. . . .

At the mouth of the bay a series of moraine islands show that the trunk glacier that occupied the bay halted here for some time and deposited this island material as a terminal moraine; that more of the bay was not filled in shows that, after lingering here, it receded comparatively fast. All the level portions of trunks of glaciers occupying ocean fiords, instead of melting back gradually in times of general shrinking and recession, as inland glaciers with sloping channels do, melt almost uniformly over all the surface until they become thin enough to float. Then, of course, with each rise and fall of the tide, the sea water, with a temperature usually considerably above the freezing-point, rushes in and out beneath them, causing rapid waste of the nether surface, while the upper is being wasted by the weather, until at length the fiord portions of these great glaciers become comparatively thin and weak and are broken up and vanish almost simultaneously.

Glacier Bay is undoubtedly young as yet. Vancouver's chart, made only a century ago, shows no trace of it, though found admirably faithful in general. It seems probable, therefore, that even then the entire bay was occupied by a glacier of which all those described above, great though they are, were only tributaries. Nearly as great a change has taken place in Sum Dum Bay since Vancouver's visit, the main trunk glacier there having receded from eighteen to twenty-five miles from the line marked on his chart. Charley, who was here when a boy, said that the place had so changed that he hardly recognized it, so many new islands had been born in the mean time and so much ice had vanished. As we have seen, this Icy Bay is being still farther extended by the recession of the glaciers. That this whole system of fiords and channels was added to the domain of the sea by glacial action is to my mind certain.

We reached the island from which we had obtained our store of fuel about half-past six and camped here for the night, having spent only five days in Sitadaka, sailing round it, visiting and sketching all the six glaciers excepting the largest, though I landed only on three of them, — the Geikie, Hugh Miller, and Grand Pacific, — the freezing of the fiords in front of the others rendering them inaccessible at this late season [pp. 158–60].

We now steered for the Muir Glacier and arrived at the front on the east side the evening of the third, and camped on the end of the moraine, where there was a small stream. Captain Tyeen was inclined to keep at a safe distance from the tremendous threatening cliffs of the discharging wall. After a good deal of urging he ventured within half a mile of them, on the east side of the fiord, where with Mr. Young I went ashore to seek a camp-ground on the moraine, leaving the Indians in the canoe. In a few minutes after we landed a huge berg sprung aloft with awful commotion, and the frightened Indians incontinently fled down the fiord, plying their paddles with admirable energy in the tossing waves until a safe harbor was reached around the south end of the moraine. I found a good place for a camp in a slight hollow where a few spruce stumps afforded firewood. But all efforts to get Tyeen out of his harbor failed. "Nobody knew," he said, "how far the angry ice mountain could throw waves to break his canoe." Therefore I had my bedding and some provisions carried to my stump camp, where I could watch the bergs as they were discharged and get night views of the brow of the glacier and its sheer jagged face all the way across from side to side of the channel. One night the water was luminous and the surge from discharging icebergs churned the water into silver fire, a glorious sight in the darkness. I also went back up the east side of the glacier five or six miles and ascended a mountain between its first two eastern tributaries, which, though covered with grass near the top, was exceedingly steep and difficult. A bulging ridge near the top I discovered was formed of ice, a remnant of the glacier when it stood at this elevation which had been preserved by moraine material and later by a thatch of dwarf bushes and grass.

Next morning at daybreak I pushed eagerly back over the comparatively smooth eastern margin of the glacier to see as much as possible of the upper fountain region. About five miles back from the front I climbed a mountain twenty-five hundred feet high, from the flowery summit of which, the day being clear, the vast glacier and its principal branches were displayed in one magnificent view. Instead of a stream of ice winding down a mountain-walled valley like the largest of the Swiss glaciers, the Muir looks like a broad undulating prairie streaked with medial moraines and gashed with crevasses, surrounded by numberless mountains from which flow its many tributary glaciers. There are seven main tributaries from ten to twenty miles long and from two to six miles wide where they enter the trunk, each of them fed by many secondary tributaries; so that the whole number of branches, great and small, pouring from the mountain fountains perhaps number upward of two hundred, not counting the smallest. The area drained by this one grand glacier can hardly be less than seven or eight hundred miles, and probably contains as much ice as all the eleven hundred Swiss glaciers combined. Its length from the frontal wall back to the head of its farthest fountain seemed to be about forty or fifty miles, and the width just below the confluence of the main tributaries about twenty-five miles. Though apparently motionless as the mountains, it flows on forever, the speed varying in every part with the seasons, but mostly with the depth of the current, and the declivity, smoothness and directness of the different portions of the basin. The flow of the central cascading portion near the front, as determined by Professor Reid, is at the rate of from two and a half to five inches an hour, or from five to ten feet a day. A strip of the main trunk about a mile in width, extending along the eastern margin about fourteen miles to a lake filled with bergs, has so little motion and is so little interrupted by crevasses, a hundred horsemen might ride abreast over it without encountering very much difficulty.

But far the greater portion of the vast expanse looking smooth in the distance is torn and crumpled into a bewildering network of hummocky ridges and blades, separated by yawning gulfs and crevasses, so that the explorer, crossing it from shore to shore, must always have a hard time. In hollow spots here and there in the heart of the icy wilderness are small lakelets fed by swift-glancing streams that flow without friction in blue shining channels, making delightful melody, singing and ringing in silvery tones of peculiar sweetness, radiant crystals like flowers ineffably fine growing in dazzling beauty along their banks. Few, however, will be likely to enjoy them. Fortunately to most travelers the thundering ice-wall, while comfortably accessible, is also the most strikingly interesting portion of the glacier.

The mountains about the great glacier were also seen from this standpoint in exceedingly grand and telling views, ranged and grouped in glorious array. Along the valleys of the main tributaries to the north-westward I saw far into their shadowy depths, one noble peak in its snowy robes appearing beyond another in fine perspective. One of the most remarkable of them, fashioned like a superb crown with delicately fluted sides, stands in the middle of the second main tributary, counting from left to right. To the westward the magnificent Fairweather Range is displayed in all its glory, lifting its peaks and glaciers into the blue sky. Mt. Fairweather, though not the highest, is the noblest and most majestic in port and architecture of all the sky-dwelling company. La Perouse, at the south end of the range, is also a magnificent mountain, symmetrically peaked and sculptured, and wears its robes of snow and glaciers in noble style. Lituya, as seen from here, is an immense tower, severely plain and massive. It makes a fine and terrible and lonely impression. Crillon, though the loftiest of all (being nearly sixteen thousand feet high), presents no well-marked features. Its ponderous glaciers have ground it away into long, curling ridges until, from this point of view, it resembles a huge twisted shell. The lower summits about the Muir Glacier, like this one, the first that I climbed, are richly adorned and enlivened with flowers, though they make but a faint show in general views. Lines and dashes of bright green appear on the lower slopes as one approaches them from the glacier, and a fainter green tinge may be noticed on the subordinate summits at a height of two thousand or three thousand feet. The lower are mostly alder bushes and the topmost a lavish profusion of flowering plants, chiefly cassiope, vaccinium, pyrola, erigeron, gentiana, campanula, anemone, larkspur, and columbine, with a few grasses and ferns. Of these cassiope is at once the commonest and the most beautiful and influential. In some places its delicate stems make mattresses more than a foot thick over several acres, while the bloom is so abundant that a single handful plucked at random contains hundreds of its pale pink bells. The very thought of this Alaska garden is a joyful exhilaration. Though the storm-beaten ground it is growing on is nearly half a mile high, the glacier centuries ago flowed over it as a river flows over a boulder; but out of all the cold darkness and glacial crushing and grinding comes this warm, abounding beauty and life to teach us that what we in our faithless ignorance and fear call destruction is creation finer and finer.

When night was approaching I scrambled down out of my blessed garden to the glacier, and returned to my lonely camp, and, getting some coffee and bread, again went up the moraine to the east end of the great ice-wall. It is about three miles long, but the length of the jagged, berg-producing portion that stretches across the fiord from side to side like a huge green-and-blue barrier is only about two miles and rises above the water to a height of from two hundred and fifty to three hundred feet. Soundings made by Captain Carroll show that seven hundred and twenty feet of the wall is below the surface, and a third unmeasured portion is buried beneath the moraine detritus deposited at the foot of it. Therefore, were the water and rocky detritus cleared away, a sheer precipice of ice would be presented nearly two miles long and more than a thousand feet high. Seen from a distance, as you come up the fiord, it seems comparatively regular in form, but it is far otherwise; bold, jagged capes jut forward into the fiord, alternating with deep reëntering angles and craggy hollows with plain bastions, while the top is roughened with innumerable spires and pyramids and sharp hacked blades leaning and toppling or cutting straight into the sky.

The number of bergs given off varies somewhat with the weather and the tides, the average being about one every five or six minutes, counting only those that roar loud enough to make themselves heard at a distance of two or three miles. The very largest, however, may under favorable conditions be heard ten miles or even farther. When a large mass sinks from the upper fissured portion of the wall, there is first a keen, prolonged, thundering roar, which slowly subsides into a low muttering growl, followed by numerous smaller grating clashing sounds from the agitated bergs that dance in the waves about the newcomer as if in welcome; and these again are followed by the swash and roar of the waves that are raised and hurled up the beach against the moraines. But the largest and most beautiful of the bergs, instead of thus falling from the upper weathered portion of the wall, rise from the submerged portion with a still grander commotion, springing with tremendous voice and gestures nearly to the top of the wall, tons of water streaming like hair down their sides, plunging and rising again and again before they finally settle in perfect poise, free at last, after having formed part of the slow-crawling glacier for centuries. And as we contemplate their history, as they sail calmly away down the fiord to the sea, how wonderful it seems that ice formed from pressed snow on the far-off mountains two or three hundred years ago should still be pure and lovely in color after all its travel and toil in the rough mountain quarries, grinding and fashioning the features of predestined landscapes.

When sunshine is sifting through the midst of the multitude of icebergs that fill the fiord and through the jets of radiant spray ever rising from the tremendous dashing and splashing of the falling and upspringing bergs, the effect is indescribably glorious. Glorious, too, are the shows they make in the night when the moon and stars are shining. The berg-thunder seems far louder than by day, and the projecting buttresses seem higher as they stand forward in the pale light, relieved by gloomy hollows, while the new-born bergs are dimly seen, crowned with faint lunar rainbows in the up-dashing spray. But it is in the darkest nights when storms are blowing and the waves are phosphorescent that the most impressive displays are made. Then the long range of ice-bluffs, unearthly splendor, luminous wave foam dashing against every bluff and drifting berg; and ever and anon amid all this wild auroral splendor some huge new-born berg dashes the living water into yet brighter foam, and the streaming torrents pouring from its sides are worn as robes of light, while they roar in awful accord with the winds and waves, deep calling unto deep, glacier to glacier, from fiord to fiord over all the wonderful bay.

After spending a few days here, we struck across to the main Hoona village on the south side of Icy Strait, thence by a long cutoff with one short portage to Chatham Strait, and thence down through Peril Strait, sailing all night, hoping to catch the mail steamer at Sitka. We arrived at the head of the strait about daybreak. The tide was falling, and rushing down with the swift current as if descending a majestic cataract was a memorable experience. We reached Sitka the same night, and there I paid and discharged my crew, making allowance for a couple of days or so for the journey back home to Fort Wrangell, while I boarded the steamer for Portland and thus ended my explorations for this season [pp. 262–70].

June 25. A rainy day. For a few hours I kept count of the number of bergs discharged, then sauntered along the beach to the end of the crystal wall. A portion of the way is dangerous, the moraine bluff being capped by an overlying lobe of the glacier, which as it melts sends down boulders and fragments of ice, while the strip of sandy shore at high tide is only a few rods wide, leaving but little room to escape from the falling moraine material and the bergwaves. The view of the ice-cliffs, pinnacles, spires

and ridges was very telling, a magnificent picture of nature's power and industry and love of beauty. About a hundred or a hundred and fifty feet from the shore a large stream issues from an arched, tunnel-like channel in the wall of the glacier, the blue of the ice hall being of an exquisite tone, contrasting with the strange, sooty, smoky, brown-colored stream. The front wall of the Muir Glacier is about two and a half or three miles wide. Only the central portion about two miles wide discharges icebergs. The two wings advanced over the washed and stratified moraine deposits have little or no motion, melting and receding as fast, or perhaps faster, than it advances. They have been advanced at least a mile over the old re-formed moraines, as is shown by the overlying, angular, recent moraine deposits, now being laid down, which are continuous with the medial moraines of the glacier.

In the old stratified banks, trunks and branches of trees showing but little sign of decay occur at a height of about a hundred feet above tidewater. I have not yet compared this fossil wood with that of the opposite shore deposits. That the glacier was once withdrawn considerably back of its present limits seems plain. Immense torrents of water had filled in the inlet with stratified moraine-material, and for centuries favorable climatic conditions allowed forests to grow upon it. At length the glacier advanced, probably three or four miles, uprooting and burying the trees which had grown undisturbed for centuries. Then came a great thaw, which produced the flood that deposited the uprooted trees. Also the trees which grew around the shores above reach of floods were shed off, perhaps by the thawing of the soil that was resting on the buried margin of the glacier, left on its re-treat and protected by a covering of moraine-material from melt-ing as fast as the exposed surface of the glacier. What appear to be remnants of the margin of the glacier when it stood at a much higher level still exist on the left side and probably all along its banks on both sides just below its present terminus.

June 26. We fixed a mark on the left wing to measure the motion if any. It rained all day, but I had a grand tramp over mud, ice, and rock to the east wall of the inlet. Brown metamorphic slate, close-grained in places, dips away from the inlet, presenting edges to ice-action, which has given rise to a singularly beautiful and striking surface, polished and grooved and fluted.

All the next day it rained. The mountains were smothered in dull-colored mist and fog, the great glacier looming through the gloomy gray fog fringes with wonderful effect. The thunder of bergs booms and rumbles through the foggy atmosphere. It is bad weather for exploring but delightful nevertheless, making all the strange, mysterious region yet stranger and more mysterious [pp. 282–84].

J*une 30.* Clearing clouds and sunshine. In less than a minute I saw three large bergs born. First there is usually a prelim-inary thundering of comparatively small masses as the large mass begins to fall, then the grand crash and boom and reverberating roaring. Oftentimes three or four heavy main throbbing thuds and booming explosions are heard as the main mass falls in several pieces, and also secondary thuds and thunderings as the mass or masses plunge and rise again and again ere they come to rest. Seldom, if ever, do the towers, battlements, and pinnacles into which the front of the glacier is broken fall forward headlong from their bases like falling trees at the water-level or above or below it. They mostly sink vertically or nearly so, as if undermined by the melting action of the water of the inlet, occasionally maintaining their upright position after sinking far below the level of the water, and rising again a hundred feet or more into the air with water streaming like hair down their sides from their crowns, then launch forward and fall flat with yet another thundering report, raising spray in magnificent, flamelike, radiating jets and sheets, occasionally to the very top of the front wall. Illumined by the sun, the spray and angular crystal masses are indescribably beautiful. Some of the discharges pour in fragments from clefts in the wall like waterfalls, white and mealy-looking, even dusty with minute swirling ice-particles, followed by a rushing succession of thunder-tones combining into a huge, blunt, solemn roar. Most of these crumbling discharges are from the excessively shattered central part of the ice-wall; the solid deep-blue masses from the ends of the wall forming the large bergs rise from the bottom of the glacier.

Many lesser reports are heard at a distance of a mile or more from the fall of pinnacles into crevasses or from the opening of new crevasses. The berg discharges are very irregular, from three to twenty-two an hour. On one rising tide, six hours, there were sixty bergs discharged, large enough to thunder and be heard at distances of from three quarters to one and a half miles; and on one succeeding falling tide, six hours, sixty-nine were discharged [pp. 285–86].

Many fine alpine plants grew here, an anemone on the summit, two species of cassiope in shaggy mats, three or four dwarf willows, large blue hairy lupines eighteen inches high, parnassia, phlox, solidago, dandelion, white-flowered bryanthus, daisy, pedicularis, epilobium, etc., with grasses, sedges, mosses, and lichens, forming a delightful deep spongy sod. Woodchucks stood erect and piped dolefully for an hour "Chee-chee!" with jaws absurdly stretched to emit so thin a note — rusty-looking, seedy fellows, also a smaller striped species which stood erect and cheeped and whistled like a Douglas squirrel. I saw three or four species of birds. A finch flew from her nest at my feet; and I almost stepped on a family of young ptarmigan ere they scattered, little bunches of downy brown silk, small but able to run well. They scattered along a snow-bank, over boulders, through willows, grass, and flowers, while the mother, very lame, tumbled and sprawled at my feet. I stood still until the little ones began to peep; the mother answered "Too-too-too" and showed admirable judgment and devotion. She was in brown plumage with white on the wing primaries. She had fine grounds on which to lead and feed her young.

Not a cloud in the sky to-day; a faint film to the north vanished by noon, leaving all the sky full of soft, hazy light. The magnificent mountains around the widespread tributaries of the glacier; the great, gently undulating, prairie-like expanse of the main trunk, bluish on the east, pure white on the west and north; its trains of moraines in magnificent curving lines and many colors — black, gray, red, and brown; the stormy, cataract-like, crevassed sections; the hundred fountains; the lofty, pure white Fairweather Range; the thunder of the plunging bergs; the fleet of bergs sailing tranquilly in the inlet — formed a glowing picture of nature's beauty and power [pp. 287–88].

I started off the morning of July 11 on my memorable sled-trip to obtain general views of the main upper part of the Muir Glacier and its seven principal tributaries, feeling sure that I would learn something and at the same time get rid of a severe bronchial cough that followed an attack of the grippe and had troubled me for three months. I intended to camp on the glacier every night, and did so, and my throat grew better every day until it was well, for no lowland microbe could stand such a trip. My sled was about three feet long and made as light as possible. A sack of hardtack, a little tea and sugar, and a sleeping-bag were firmly lashed on it so that nothing could drop off however much it might be jarred and dangled in crossing crevasses.

Two Indians carried the baggage over the rocky moraine to the clear glacier at the side of one of the eastern Nunatak Islands. Mr. Loomis accompanied me to this first camp and assisted in dragging the empty sled over the moraine. We arrived at the middle

Travels in Alaska

Nunatak Island about nine o'clock. Here I sent back my Indian carriers, and Mr. Loomis assisted me the first day in hauling the loaded sled to my second camp at the foot of Hemlock Mountain, returning the next morning.

July 13. I skirted the mountain to eastward a few miles and was delighted to discover a group of trees high up on its ragged rocky side, the first trees I had seen on the shores of Glacier Bay or on those of any of its glaciers. I left my sled on the ice and climbed the mountain to see what I might learn. I found that all the trees were mountain hemlock (*Tsuga mertensiana*), and were evidently the remnant of an old well-established forest, standing on the only ground that was stable, all the rest of the forest below it having been sloughed off with the soil from the disintegrating slate bed rock. The lowest of the trees stood at an elevation of about two thousand feet above the sea, the highest at about three thousand feet or a little higher. Nothing could be more striking than the contrast between the raw, crumbling, deforested portions of the mountain, looking like a quarry that was being worked, and the forested part with its rich, shaggy beds of cassiope and bryanthus in full bloom, and its sumptuous cushions of flower-enameled mosses. These garden-patches are full of gay colors of gentian, erigeron, anemone, larkspur, and columbine, and are enlivened with happy birds and bees and marmots. Climbing to an elevation of twenty-five hundred feet, which is about fifteen hundred feet above the level of the glacier at this point, I saw and heard a few marmots, and three ptarmigans that were as tame as barnyard fowls. The sod is sloughing off on the edges, keeping it ragged. The trees are stormbent from the southeast. A few are standing at an elevation of nearly three thousand feet; at twenty-five hundred feet, pyrola, veratrum, vaccinium, fine grasses, sedges, willows, mountain-ash, buttercups, and acres of the most luxuriant cassiope are in bloom.

A lake encumbered with icebergs lies at the end of Divide Glacier. A spacious, level-floored valley beyond it, eight or ten miles long, with forested mountains on its west side, perhaps discharges to the southeastward into Lynn Canal. The divide of the glacier is about opposite the third of the eastern tributaries. Another berg-dotted lake into which the drainage of the Braided Glacier flows, lies a few miles to the westward and is one and a half miles long. Berg Lake is next the remarkable Girdled Glacier to the southeastward.

When the ice-period was in its prime, much of the Muir Glacier that now flows northward into Howling Valley flowed southward into Glacier Bay as a tributary of the Muir. All the rock contours show this, and so do the medial moraines. Berg Lake is crowded with bergs because they have no outlet and melt slowly. I heard none discharged. I had a hard time crossing the Divide Glacier, on which I camped. Half a mile back from the lake I gleaned a little fossil wood and made a fire on moraine boulders for tea. I slept fairly well on the sled. I heard the roar of four cascades on a shaggy green mountain on the west side of Howling Valley and saw three wild goats fifteen hundred feet up in the steep grassy pastures [pp. 294–96].

Travels in Alaska

It has been a glorious day, all pure sunshine. An hour or more before sunset the distant mountains, a vast host, seemed more softly ethereal than ever, pale blue, ineffably fine, all angles and harshness melted off in the soft evening light. Even the snow and the grinding, cascading glaciers became divinely tender and fine in this celestial amethystine light. I got back to camp at 7:15, not tired. After my hardtack supper I could have climbed the mountain again and got back before sunrise, but dragging the sled tires me. I have been out on the glacier examining a moraine-like mass about a third of a mile from camp. It is perhaps a mile long, a hundred yards wide, and is thickly strewn with wood. I think that it has been brought down the mountain by a heavy snow avalanche, loaded on the ice, then carried away from the shore in the direction of the flow of the glacier. This explains detached moraine-masses. This one seems to have been derived from a big roomy cirque or amphitheatre on the northwest side of this Snow Dome Mountain.

To shorten the return journey I was tempted to glissade down what appeared to be a snow-filled ravine, which was very steep. All went well until I reached a bluish spot which proved to be ice, on which I lost control of myself and rolled into a gravel talus at the foot without a scratch. Just as I got up and was getting myself orientated, I heard a loud fierce scream, uttered in an exulting, diabolical tone of voice which startled me, as if an enemy, having seen me fall, was glorying in my death. Then suddenly two ravens came swooping from the sky and alighted on the jag of a rock within a few feet of me, evidently hoping that I had been maimed and that they were going to have a feast. But as they stared at me, studying my condition, impatiently waiting for bone-picking time, I saw what they were up to and shouted, "Not yet, not yet!"

July 16. At 7 A.M. I left camp to cross the main glacier. Six ravens came to the camp as soon as I left. What wonderful eyes they must have! Nothing that moves in all this icy wilderness escapes the eyes of these brave birds. This is one of the loveliest mornings I ever saw in Alaska; not a cloud or faintest hint of one in all the wide sky. There is a yellowish haze in the east, white in the west, mild and mellow as a Wisconsin Indian Summer, but finer, more ethereal, God's holy light making all divine.

In an hour or so I came to the confluence of the first of the seven grand tributaries of the main Muir Glacier and had a glorious view of it as it comes sweeping down in wild cascades from its magnificent, pure white, mountain-girt basin to join the main crystal sea, its many fountain peaks, clustered and crowded, all pouring forth their tribute to swell its grand current. I crossed its front a little below its confluence, where its shattered current, about two or three miles wide, is reunited, and many rills and good-sized brooks glide gurgling and ringing in pure blue channels, giving delightful animation to the icy solitude.

Most of the ice-surface crossed to-day has been very uneven, and hauling the sled and finding a way over hummocks has been fatiguing. At times I had to lift the sled bodily and to cross many narrow, nerve-trying, ice-sliver bridges, balancing astride of them, and cautiously shoving the sled ahead of me with tremendous chasms on either side. I had made perhaps not more than six or eight miles in a straight line by six o'clock, this evening when I reached ice so hummocky and tedious I concluded to camp and not try to take the sled any farther. I intend to leave it here in the middle of the basin and carry my sleeping-bag and provisions the rest of the way across to the west side. I am cozy and comfortable here resting in the midst of glorious icy scenery, though very tired. I made out to get a cup of tea by means of a few shavings and splinters whittled from the bottom board of my sled, and made a fire in a little can, a small campfire, the smallest I ever made or saw, yet it answered well enough as far as tea was concerned. I crept into my sack before eight o'clock as the wind was cold and my feet wet. One of my shoes is about worn out. I may have to put on a wooden sole. This day has been cloudless throughout, with lovely sunshine, a purple evening and morning. The circumference of mountains beheld from the midst of this world of ice is marvelous, the vast plain reposing in such soft tender light, the fountain mountains so clearly cut, holding themselves aloft with their loads of ice in supreme strength and beauty of architecture. I found a skull and most of the other bones of a goat on the glacier about two miles from the nearest land. It had probably been chased out of its mountain home by wolves and devoured here. I carried its horns with me. I saw many considerable depressions in the glacial surface, also a pitlike hole, irregular, not like the ordinary wells along the slope of the many small dirt-clad hillocks, faced to the south. Now the sun is down and the sky is saffron yellow, blending and fading into purple around to the south and north. It is a curious experience to be lying in bed writing these notes, hummock waves rising in every direction, their edges marking a multitude of crevasses and pits, while all around the horizon rise peaks innumerable of most intricate style of architecture. Solemnly growling and grinding moulins contrast with the sweet low-voiced whispering and warbling of a network of rills, singing like water-ouzels, glinting, gliding with indescribable softness and sweetness of voice. They are all around, one within a few feet of my hard sled bed.

July 17. Another glorious cloudless day is dawning in yellow and purple and soon the sun over the eastern peak will blot out the blue peak shadows and make all the vast white ice prairie sparkle. I slept well last night in the middle of the icy sea. The wind was cold but my sleeping-bag enabled me to lie neither warm nor intolerably cold. My three-months cough is gone. Strange that with such work and exposure one should know nothing of sore throats and of what are called colds. My heavy, thick-soled shoes, resoled just before starting on the trip six days ago, are about worn out and my feet have been wet every night. But no harm comes of it, nothing but good. I succeeded in getting a warm breakfast in bed. I reached over the edge of my sled, got hold of a small cedar stick that I had been carrying, whittled a lot of thin shavings from it, stored them on my breast, then set fire to a piece of paper in a shallow tin can, added a pinch of shavings, held the cup of water that always stood at my bedside over the tiny blaze with one hand, and fed the fire by adding little pinches of shavings until the water boiled, then pulling my bread sack within reach, made a good warm breakfast, cooked and eaten in bed. Thus refreshed, I surveyed the wilderness of crevassed, hummocky ice and concluded to try to drag my little sled a mile or two farther, then, finding encouragement, persevered, getting it across innumerable crevasses and streams and around several lakes and over and through the midst of hummocks, and at length reached the western shore between five and six o'clock this evening, extremely fatigued. This I consider a hard job well done, crossing so wildly broken a glacier, fifteen miles of it from Snow Dome Mountain, in two days with a sled weighing altogether not less than a hundred pounds. I found innumerable crevasses, some of them brimful of water. I crossed in most places just where the ice was close pressed and welded after descending cascades and was being shoved over an upward slope, thus closing the crevasses at the bottom, leaving only the upper sunmelted beveled portion open for water to collect in.

Vast must be the drainage from this great basin. The waste in sunshine must be enormous, while in dark weather rains and winds also melt the ice and add to the volume produced by the rain itself. The winds also, though in temperature they may be only a degree or two above freezing-point, dissolve the ice as fast, or perhaps faster, than clear sunshine. Much of the water caught in tight crevasses doubtless freezes during the winter and gives rise to many of the irregular veins seen in the structure of the glacier. Saturated snow also freezes at times and is incorporated with the ice, as only from the lower part of the glacier is the snow melted during the summer. I have noticed many traces of this action. One of the most beautiful things to be seen on the glacier is the myriads of minute and intensely brilliant radiant lights burning in rows on the banks of streams and pools and lakelets from the tips of crystals melting in the sun, making them look as if bordered with diamonds. These gems are rayed like stars and twinkle; no diamond radiates keener or more brilliant light. It was perfectly glorious to think of this divine light burning over all this vast crystal sea in such ineffably fine effulgence, and over how many other of icy Alaska's glaciers where nobody sees it. To produce these effects I fancy the ice must be melting rapidly, as it was being melted to-day. The ice in these pools does not melt with anything like an even surface, but in long branches and leaves, making fairy forests of points, while minute bubbles of air are constantly being set free. I am camped to-night on what I call Quarry Mountain from its raw, loose, plantless condition, seven or eight miles above the front of the glacier. I found enough fossil wood for tea. Glorious is the view to the eastward from this camp. The sun has set, a few clouds appear, and a torrent rushing down a gully and under the edge of the glacier is making a solemn roaring. No tinkling, whistling rills this night. Ever and anon I hear a falling boulder. I have had a glorious and instructive day, but am excessively weary and to bed I go.

July 18. I felt tired this morning and meant to rest to-day. But after breakfast at 8 A.M. I felt I must be up and doing, climbing, sketching new views up the great tributaries from the top of Quarry Mountain. Weariness vanished and I could have climbed, I think, five thousand feet. Anything seems easy after sled-dragging over hummocks and crevasses, and the constant nerve-strain in jumping crevasses so as not to slip in making the spring. Quarry Mountain is the barest I have seen, a raw quarry with infinite abundance of loose decaying granite all on the go. Its slopes are excessively steep. A few patches of epilobium make gay purple spots of color. Its seeds fly everywhere seeking homes. Quarry Mountain is cut across into a series of parallel ridges by oversweeping ice. It is still overswept in three places by glacial flows a half to three quarters of a mile wide, finely arched at the top of the divides. I have been sketching, though my eyes are much inflamed and I can scarce see. All the lines I make appear double. I fear I shall not be able to make the few more sketches I want to-morrow, but must try. The day has been gloriously sunful, the glacier pale yellow toward five o'clock. The hazy air, white with a yellow tinge, gives an Indian-summerish effect. Now the blue evening shadows are creeping out over the icy plain, some ten miles long, with sunny yellow belts between them. Boulders fall now and again with dull, blunt blooming, and the gravel pebbles rattle.

July 19. Nearly blind. The light is intolerable and I fear I may be long unfitted for work. I have been lying on my back all day with a snow poultice bound over my eyes. Every object I try to look at sees double; even the distant mountain-ranges are doubled, the upper an exact copy of the lower, though somewhat faint. This is the first time in Alaska that I have had too much sunshine. About four o'clock this afternoon, when I was waiting for the evening shadows to enable me to get nearer the main camp, where I could be more easily found in case my eyes should become still more inflamed and I should be unable to travel, thin clouds cast a grateful shade over all the glowing landscape. I gladly took advantage of these kindly clouds to make an effort to cross the few miles of the glacier that lay between me and the shore of the inlet. I made a pair of goggles but am afraid to wear them. Fortunately the ice here is but little broken, therefore I pulled my cap well down and set off about five o'clock. I got on pretty well and camped on the glacier in sight of the main camp, which from here in a straight line is only five or six miles away. I went ashore on Granite Island and gleaned a little fossil wood with which I made tea on the ice.

July 20. I kept wet bandages on my eyes last night as long as I could, and feel better this morning, but all the mountains still seem to have double summits, giving a curiously unreal aspect to the landscape. I packed everything on the sled and moved three miles farther down the glacier, where I want to make measurements. Twice to-day I was invited on the ice by a hummingbird, attracted by the red lining of the bearskin sleeping-bag.

I have gained some light on the formation of gravel-beds along the inlet. The material is mostly sifted and sorted by successive rollings and washings along the margins of the glacier-tributaries, where the supply is abundant beyond anything I ever saw elsewhere. The lowering of the surface of a glacier when its walls are not too steep leaves a part of the margin dead and buried and protected from the wasting sunshine beneath the lateral moraines. Thus a marginal valley is formed, clear ice on one side, or nearly so, buried ice on the other. As melting goes on, the marginal trough, or valley, grows deeper and wider, since both sides are being melted, the land side slower. The dead, protected ice in melting first sheds off the large boulders, as they are not able to lie on slopes where smaller ones can. Then the next larger ones are rolled off, and pebbles and sand in succession. Meanwhile this material is subjected to torrent-action, as if it were cast into a trough. When floods come it is carried forward and stratified, according to the force of the current, sand, mud, or larger material. This exposes fresh surfaces of ice and melting goes on again, until enough material has been undermined to form a veil in front; then follows another washing and carrying-away and depositing where the current is allowed to spread. In melting, protected margin terraces are oftentimes formed. Perhaps these terraces mark successive heights of the glacial surface. From terrace to terrace the grist of stone is rolled and sifted. Some, meeting only feeble streams, have only the fine particles carried away and deposited in smooth beds; others, coarser, from swifter streams, overspread the fine beds, while many of the large boulders no doubt roll back upon the glacier to go on their travels again.

It has been cloudy mostly to-day, though sunny in the afternoon, and my eyes are getting better. The steamer Queen is expected in a day or two, so I must try to get down to the inlet to-morrow and make signal to have some of the Reid party ferry me over. I must hear from home, write letters, get rest and more to eat.

Near the front of the glacier the ice was perfectly free, apparently, of anything like a crevasse, and in walking almost carelessly down it I stopped opposite the large granite Nunatak Island, thinking that I would there be partly sheltered from the wind. I had not gone a dozen steps toward the island when I suddenly dropped into a concealed water-filled crevasse, which on the surface showed not the slightest sign of its existence. This crevasse like many others was being used as the channel of a stream, and at some narrow point the small cubical masses of ice into which the glacier surface disintegrates were jammed and extended back farther and farther till they completely covered and concealed the water. Into this I suddenly plunged, after crossing thousands of really dangerous crevasses, but never before had I encountered a danger so completely concealed. Down I plunged over head and ears, but of course bobbed up again, and after a hard struggle succeeded in dragging myself out over the farther side. Then I pulled my sled over close to Nunatak cliff, made haste to strip off my clothing, threw it in a sloppy heap and crept into my sleeping-bag to shiver away the night as best I could.

July 21. Dressing this rainy morning was a miserable job, but might have been worse. After wringing my sloppy underclothing, getting it on was far from pleasant. My eyes are better and I feel no bad effect from my icy bath. The last trace of my three months' cough is gone. No lowland grippe microbe could survive such experiences.

I have had a fine telling day examining the ruins of the old forest of Sitka spruce that no great time ago grew in a shallow mud-filled basin near the southwest corner of the glacier. The trees were protected by a spur of the mountain that puts out here, and when the glacier advanced they were simply flooded with fine sand and overborne. Stumps by the hundred, three to fifteen feet high, rooted in a stream of fine blue mud on cobbles, still have their bark on. A stratum of decomposed bark, leaves, cones, and old trunks is still in place. Some of the stumps are on rocky ridges of gravelly soil about one hundred and twenty-five feet above the sea. The valley has been washed out by the stream now occupying it, one of the glacier's draining streams a mile long or more and an eighth of a mile wide.

I got supper early and was just going to bed, when I was startled by seeing a man coming across the moraine, Professor Reid, who had seen me from the main camp and who came with Mr. Loomis and the cook in their boat to ferry me over. I had not intended making signals for them until to-morrow but was glad to go. I had been seen also by Mr. Case and one of his companions, who were on the western mountain-side above the fossil forest, shooting ptarmigans. I had a good rest and sleep and leisure to find out how rich I was in new facts and pictures and how tired and hungry I was [pp. 299–311].

With the utmost caution I picked my way through the sparkling bergs, and after an hour or two of this nerve-trying work, when I was perhaps less than halfway across and dreading the loss of the frail canoe which would include the loss of myself, I came to a pack of very large bergs which loomed threateningly, offering no visible thoroughfare. Paddling and pushing to right and left, I at last discovered a sheer-walled opening about four feet wide and perhaps two hundred feet long, formed apparently by the splitting of a huge iceberg. I hesitated to enter this passage, fearing that the slightest change in the tide-current might close it, but ventured nevertheless, judging that the dangers ahead might not be greater than those I had already passed. When I had got about a third of the way in, I suddenly discovered that the smooth-walled ice-lane was growing narrower, and with desperate haste backed out. Just as the bow of the canoe cleared the sheer walls they came together with a growling crunch. Terror-stricken, I turned back, and in an anxious hour or two gladly reached the rock-bound shore that had at first repelled me, determined to stay on guard all night in the canoe or find some place where with the strength that comes in a fight for life I could drag it up the boulder wall beyond ice danger. This at last was happily done about midnight, and with no thought of sleep I went to bed rejoicing.

My bed was two boulders, and as I lay wedged and bent on their up-bulging sides, beguiling the hard, cold time in gazing into the starry sky and across the sparkling bay, magnificent upright bars of light in bright prismatic colors suddenly appeared, marching swiftly in close succession along the northern horizon from west to east as if in diligent haste, an auroral display very different from any I had ever before beheld. Once long ago in Wisconsin I saw the heavens draped in rich purple auroral clouds fringed and folded in most magnificent forms; but in this glory of light, so pure, so bright, so enthusiastic in motion, there was nothing in the least cloud-like. The short color-bars, apparently about two degrees in height, though blending, seemed to be as well defined as those of the solar spectrum.

How long these glad, eager soldiers of light held on their way I cannot tell; for sense of time was charmed out of mind and the blessed night circled away in measureless rejoicing enthusiasm.

In the early morning after so inspiring a night I launched my canoe feeling able for anything, crossed the mouth of the Hugh Miller fiord, and forced a way three or four miles along the shore of the bay, hoping to reach the Grand Pacific Glacier in front of Mt. Fairweather. But the farther I went, the ice-pack, instead of showing inviting little open streaks here and there, became so much harder jammed that on some parts of the shore the bergs, drifting south with the tide, was shoving one another out of the water beyond high-tide line. Farther progress to northward was thus rigidly stopped, and now I had to fight for a way back to my cabin, hoping that by good tide luck I might reach it before dark. But at sundown I was less than half-way home, and though very hungry was glad to land on a little rock island with a smooth beach for the canoe and a thicket of alder bushes for fire and bed and a little sleep. But shortly after sundown, while these arrangements were being made, lo and behold another aurora enriching the heavens! and though it proved to be one of the ordinary almost colorless kind, thrusting long, quivering lances toward the zenith from a dark cloud-like base, after last night's wonderful display one's expectations might well be extravagant and I lay wide awake watching.

On the third night I reached my cabin and food. Professor

John Muir

Reid and his party came in to talk over the results of our excursions, and just as the last one of the visitors opened the door after bidding good-night, he shouted, "Muir, come look here. Here's something fine."

I ran out in auroral excitement, and sure enough here was another aurora, as novel and wonderful as the marching rainbow-colored columns — a glowing silver bow spanning the Muir Inlet in a magnificent arch right under the zenith, or a little to the south of it, the ends resting on the top of the mountain-walls. And though colorless and steadfast, its intense, solid, white splendor, noble proportions, and fineness of finish excited boundless admiration. In form and proportion it was like a rainbow, a bridge of one span five miles wide; and so brilliant, so fine and solid and homogeneous in every part, I fancy that if all the stars were raked together into one windrow, fused and welded and run through some celestial rolling-mill, all would be required to make this one glowing white colossal bridge.

After my last visitor went to bed, I lay down on the moraine in front of the cabin and gazed and watched. Hour after hour the wonderful arch stood perfectly motionless, sharply defined and substantial-looking as if it were a permanent addition to the furniture of the sky. At length while it yet spanned the inlet in serene unchanging splendor, a band of fluffy, pale gray, quivering ringlets came suddenly all in a row over the eastern mountain-top, glided in nervous haste up and down the under side of the bow and over the western mountain-wall. They were about one and a half times the apparent diameter of the bow in length, maintained a vertical posture all the way across, and slipped swiftly along as if they were suspended like a curtain on rings. Had these lively auroral fairies marched across the fiord on the top of the bow instead of shuffling along the under side of it, one might have fancied they were a happy band of spirit people on a journey making use of the splendid bow for a bridge. There must have been hundreds of miles of them; for the time required for each to cross from one end of the bridge to the other seemed only a minute or less, while nearly an hour elapsed from their first appearance until the last of the rushing throng vanished behind the western mountain, leaving the bridge as bright and solid and steadfast as before they arrived. But later, half an hour or so, it began to fade. Fissures or cracks crossed it diagonally through which a few stars were seen, and gradually it became thin and nebulous until it looked like the Milky Way, and at last vanished, leaving no visible monument of any sort to mark its place.

I now returned to my cabin, replenished the fire, warmed myself, and prepared to go to bed, though too aurorally rich and happy to go to sleep. But just as I was about to retire, I thought I had better take another look at the sky, to make sure that the glorious show was over; and, contrary to all reasonable expectations, I found that the pale foundation for another bow was being laid right overhead like the first. Then losing all thought of sleep, I ran back to my cabin, carried out blankets and lay down on the moraine to keep watch until daybreak, that none of the sky wonders of the glorious night within reach of my eyes might be lost.

I had seen the first bow when it stood complete in full splendor, and its gradual fading decay. Now I was to see the building of a new one from the beginning. Perhaps in less than half an hour the silvery material was gathered, condensed, and welded into a glowing, evenly proportioned arc like the first and in the same part of the sky. Then in due time over the eastern mountain-wall came another throng of restless electric auroral fairies, the infinitely fine pale-gray garments of each lightly touching those of their neighbors as they swept swiftly along the under side of the bridge and down over the western mountain like the merry band that had gone the same way before them, all keeping quivery step and time to music too fine for mortal ears.

While the gay throng was gliding swiftly along, I watched the bridge for any change they might make upon it, but not the slightest could I detect. They left no visible track, and after all had passed the glowing arc stood firm and apparently immutable, but at last faded slowly away like its glorious predecessor.

Excepting only the vast purple aurora mentioned above, said to have been visible over nearly all the continent, these two silver bows in supreme, serene, supernal beauty surpassed everything auroral I ever beheld [pp. 313–18].